"Prepare to be challenged in every
fixating on superficial structur..
underlying spiritual qualities needed for authentic change in the church."

— *Dennis McCallum, author and Founder/Lead Pastor of
Xenos Christian Fellowship, Columbus, OH*

" 'Please allow me to be blunt (again).' That's one of my favorite lines
from this book, and I hope you will honor Randall's request and allow
him to speak truthfully—even bluntly—into your experiences with small
group ministry. Like any good doctor, Randall's words will prod areas of
weakness and poor judgment, but in the end he offers good medicine."

— *Sam O'Neal, Managing Editor, www.smallgroups.com,
Christianity Today International*

"Every movement loses her way. Then God brings someone along to
redirect that movement back to her roots. This book not only reminds the
small group world who she must become again but also gives practical
advice on how to return there. If your small group ministry is struggling,
you are considering starting a small group ministry, or you've tried small
groups before and come up lacking, this book was written for you!"

— *Rick Howerton, author and National Director of Events and Training,
Serendipity by Lifeway*

"Through the last 12 years of working very closely with Randall, I know
one thing for sure: I'll always get an honest answer from him. And this is
exactly what you'll find in *The Naked Truth about Small Groups*. Randall
reveals what has gone wrong with small groups in North America. But he
doesn't stop there. He offers biblical solutions that will help transform
you, your church, and your small groups."

— *Joel Comiskey, author, Lead Pastor of Wellspring Church, Moreno Valley, CA
and President, Joel Comiskey Group*

"Randall exposes the raw facts about small group ministry while revealing God's original designs for both living out the great commandment and carrying out the great commission. *The Naked Truth About Small Group Ministry* is chock-full of practical wisdom, problem-solving paradigms, and a genuine passion for missional communities of faith, love, and hope."

— *Dave Auda, Small Groups Pastor, Mosaic, Los Angeles, CA*

"The first step towards healing is admitting that you have a problem. And if we aren't willing to admit the problem, Randall Neighbour is bold enough to do it for us. Standing on years of experience, Neighbour shoots straight with pictures, stories, and raw reflections on the state of community and discipleship in our churches, and offers straightforward and time-tested advice for getting back to Biblical basics. Like a good athletic trainer, he breaks us down in order to build us up to greater strength."

—*Heather Zempel, Discipleship Pastor, National Community Church, Washington, D.C.*

"I love Randall Neighbour, but he irritates me. It must be his spiritual gift. He exposes why some of our cherished methods and practices fail: they're unsatisfactory, unrealistic, and sometimes unbiblical—but we keep doing them anyway! We'd go right on doing them, too, without this discerning and gifted practitioner screaming: *The emperor has no clothes!* Well known within the cell-church community, Randall's insights are informed by years of experience and a love of Christ and his Church. His ministry framework may not precisely overlap your own, but his insights apply to anyone who wants to facilitate the formation of true Biblical community. If your small group ministry is thriving, on life-support or even left for dead, this book can show you why, and what to do next."

—*Dave Treat, Group Life Speaker, Trainer, and Writer, thinkingsmall.net*

"If you are looking for nice platitudes or easy advice about small groups, you won't get them here. Randall has been around the 'small group block' too many times to ignore the fact that groups are about real people and messy relationships in the real world. If you want sound counsel on how to deal with the realities of these kinds of people and their relationships, then find the time to devour this book."

—*Scott Boren, pastor, consultant, and author of*
The Relational Way *and* Missional Small Groups

THE
NAKED TRUTH
ABOUT
SMALL GROUP
MINISTRY

THE
NAKED TRUTH
ABOUT
SMALL GROUP
MINISTRY

When it
won't
work
and what
to do
about it

Randall Neighbour

TOUCH
Publications
Houston, Texas

TOUCH® Publications
P.O. Box 7847
Houston, Texas, 77270, U.S.A.
800-735-5865 • www.touchusa.org

Cover design by Neubauer Design Group

International Standard Book Number: 978-0-9788779-6-5

TOUCH® Publications is the book-publishing division
of TOUCH Outreach Ministries, a resource and consulting ministry for
churches with a vision for a holistic small group-based church structure.

Find TOUCH® on the web at: http://www.touchusa.org

Visit the author's blog: http://www.randallneighbour.com

To Mom and Dad
Thank you for the inheritance of a passion for Christ.

CONTENTS

I oversee a ministry that was founded to help churches implement holistic small groups with consulting, training, and printed resources. Today, TOUCH Outreach has ministry partners in South Korea, Brazil, Hong Kong, South Africa, Australia, and Eastern Europe. In each of these areas of the world, my counterparts report that small-group-based churches are growing rapidly with new believers and new leaders, validating my own observations about a global shift away from buildings and programs.

The members of these churches are very active believers who—in small group families—pray fervently, serve sacrificially, and worship boldly. These small groups grow and multiply regularly through mentoring new Christians and new leaders, causing all sorts of wonderful challenges for the pastoral staff, especially in the areas of discipleship and leadership training.

Here in America, reports from pastors with whom I visit are in stark contrast to the rest of the world. While many American churches are growing numerically when counting noses on Sunday morning, I consistently hear comments such as, "No one wants to lead a group because they're too busy" or "We can't seem to get our cell groups to focus on reaching unchurched people for Christ" or "Our small group ministry just isn't growing like other churches we read about."

One might think this malady is only found in smaller, struggling churches. Not so! America's largest churches are not seeing their small groups multiply naturally through relationships. Most increase the number of groups with hastily formed collections of interested strangers.

As a nation of church leaders desiring true biblical community, we've got a big problem with small groups.

The relational counterculture

The typical American pastor struggles to make small groups work. Each small gain made in small group life is a hard-fought battle. The traditional church culture still holds back many lay leaders who are heavily invested in antiquated programs. There is simply no room to belong to or lead a small group into Christ's presence, power, and purposes for their lives.

Those who have broken out of the traditional church roles to lead small groups remain so busy with career and family that they do not have time to devote to relationships with group members between meetings. Moreover, small group members, who are fully capable of leading a group, have no desire to lead because of greater priorities. Little League baseball games and working a high-stress job to serve a growing debt load are far more important than living and ministering to others in biblical community.

The two conflicting cultures in which we live—found inside and outside the walls of church buildings—work against the formation of a third *relational* counterculture, where Christ's presence births personal transformation in the midst of a small group family. Attempting to move one's congregation out of one unresolved cultural clash into a strange new way of life is no easy task. The road to outward-focused biblical community will no doubt be awash with the blood, sweat, and tears of many hard-working pastors.

We're not good at doing small groups, but we value small groups.

Aside from the stark global comparison and cultural concerns mentioned, I remain confident that a sizeable percentage of American church leaders would say they value small groups. Each is sacrificially working to make small groups thrive in the western world.

A few have given up, but most pastors keep trying, and for good reason: "doing church" in small groups is biblical. Small groups can easily achieve both the Great Commandment (Mark 12:30) and Great Commission (Matthew 28:18-20). Small groups and weekend services also mirror the balance we find in the early church, as described in Acts 2 where the early Christians met from house to house (the small group) and in the temple courts (the weekend service). The quest to pastor a church of healthy, Christ-centered, mission-driven small groups is indeed a holy pursuit.

I grew up in a small-group-based church. My father pioneered "cell groups" here in America in the early 1970s when I was in grade school. I cut my teeth on leadership when I became a cell group leader as a teen. The first year I led a group, seven of my buddies came to Christ, four led groups the next year, and one went on to seminary after college. I value small groups so much that I've devoted my life to helping churches launch and transition to small-group-based expressions of the body of Christ.

In the last ten years, I have read everything I can get my hands on that is related to small groups or small group ministry. If a book can teach me one new thing or give me a single "aha!" moment about doing church through biblical community, it is worth buying and reading. I also fly around the country to attend conferences when the focus is on small-group-based ministry. While this is time-consuming and often expensive, I value small groups enough to pursue answers to my hard questions. Why are American Christians so weak at living and serving in biblical community? And more importantly, what should be done to change it?

If you are as militant as I in this quest, we are kindred spirits. Together, we must clearly see the problems, fix what's broken, and retire what no longer works. At the end of the day, we may have to simply scrap everything and start over with new small groups that grow and expand naturally. I don't relish the idea of starting over, but we've got to get this right.

How and why I define "small groups"

On page 18, you will read my definition of a small group. This book is written with this kind of group in mind. If you want more (or better) Bible study groups, DVD-curriculum-based groups, Sunday school classes, or task-based groups (parking lot attendants groups, usher's groups, bus ministry worker's groups, and so on), you are reading the *wrong* book.

The small group I am passionate about operates as *Christ's bride*. When the members of these groups look in a mirror, they see a minister with a ministry. They know without a doubt that God has placed them in a small group of believers to live out their spiritual purpose. They look to their pastor and church leaders to equip and assist them in doing what Christ has directed them to do: extend the kingdom of God. This book is written to help church leaders create healthy, spiritual organisms … small groups of believers who know they are the church in action and are eager to work hard in the harvest fields.

Is this what you're looking for in your small groups? If so, then you're reading the right book. If you're highly frustrated with small group ministry, it's also the right *time* to read this book. People don't make radical changes until they become emotional about their current situation.

Who'd have dreamed that guy was talking about a bridge failure...

The end is near!

Guys like the one in the cartoon above are ignored because people think they're crazy. This guy doesn't work for the county civil engineering department, and he's certainly not out by the side of the road in an official, respected capacity.

I am just like that unkempt man on the side of the road communicating a simple, yet important message to anyone who passes. This book is my cardboard sign for the road you are traveling, admonishing you to move forward cautiously and consider a new road that does not end abruptly. Detours always take more time and are both frustrating and unexpected. However, the new route has been designed to move the drivers around the obstacles and get them on their way toward their original destination. Unlike the guy in the cartoon, I also provide a few practical ways to detour the road on which your church may be traveling.

Many churches have found these ideas helpful. If you can use them, great! If they spark ideas for your own innovative ways to avoid the bridge failures in small group ministry you are experiencing, that's even better. The goal is to achieve God's desired destination: personal transformation through the power of Christ-centered community. ◆

The author's definition of a holistic small group with the potential for organic growth and multiplication is as follows:

> A healthy small group is comprised of 3-12 persons who have chosen to live together in biblical community for the purposes of Christ-centered worship, edification, relational evangelism, and discipleship.

The *ministry* between group members is found both inside and outside the meetings as they serve, pray, care for, and edify one another. Small group meetings are often a "discovery time" for ministry in the six days and twenty-two hours between gatherings.

The *mission* of a healthy small group takes place when two or more of the members befriend unchurched individuals to show them the love of Christ through friendship, servanthood, and community involvement.

The *goal* of a healthy small group is to help each member find personal transformation in Christ. When transformation takes place in the life of a believer, he or she discovers a new self-perception in being a minister and a missionary.

The *results* of a healthy small group are found in its fruits: members who walk in spiritual freedom and are mission-driven; the addition of new believers who have trusted Christ as a result of the group's relational nature; and new leaders who desire to first serve as new group leaders, then go on to lead in every capacity God desires.

In healthy small groups, the leader's overarching goal for each member is similar to a parent. His or her desire is to see the members mature to the point of moving out of the leader's "house" to form a spiritual family of their own. Healthy small group leaders work toward and expect a legacy from their efforts and dedication. In turn, the members desire to exercise their spiritual maturity and lead a group when they are ready.

Small groups may meet in any location and at any time. The important factor is for the group to meet regularly for worship, edification, application of the Word, and planning for effective outreach to the lost. Healthy small groups are compelled to change the location, frequency, or time of meetings if they see any of these purposes suffering.

Healthy small groups, as defined here, are called by many names. Some churches call them life groups, cell groups, small groups, care groups, or home groups ... just to name a few. The accomplishments of a healthy small group of believers are what is important. Therefore, you will read accounts of small groups using many names in this book. ◆

There's a house on a hill and it hasn't been lived in for a long, long time.
And the windows are all broken, and the paint has lost its shine.
And there's nothing ever heard there, for there's nothing ever said.
For the life of the house left a long time ago and the heart of the house is dead.

O House of the Lord, can't you feel it? How our heart is growing cold.
For when the Spirit comes He quickens, but when the Spirit leaves, life goes.

There's a room at the top and the door has been locked and it will never open up.
For no matter who will knock there, well it always stays tight shut.
And there's no-one ever answered, so now there's no-one ever goes.
For the room in the house shut a long time ago, and the mind of the house is closed.

There's a room in the house where the fire used to burn and the children used to play.
And the family would gather, to hear the words the Father would say.
But now the room is cold and empty, and the embers glow faint red,
For the fire of the house failed a long time ago, and the heart of the house is dead.

CHAPTER ONE

The naked truth about the American church: the heart of the house is dead

Why do small groups so frequently not work in the West? The answer is rather obvious: the members of the groups are consumers. They do not currently possess a passion for God or for those for whom his Son died. Therefore, small groups aren't a structure that the members value. It requires them to produce.

This is compounded by the typical way these small groups were formed by church leadership. Members were herded into the new small group program and instructed to study the Bible, care for one another, worship, or reach out to the unchurched world with little consideration for their current spiritual condition.

When one stops to ponder the viability of the herding approach, it's not hard to see why so many churches fail to implement healthy groups. "Corralling" church members into small groups so they will then live out their faith together in community is not only unrealistic, it's absurd. It maintains the same pretzel logic I followed years ago when I joined a gym. I paid my dues, received my laminated card, and carved out the time to go to that gym three times a week. My hope was to lose all the weight I gained during my first ten years of marriage. With my membership and renewed self-discipline, each Monday, Wednesday, and Saturday I soaked in the whirlpool and sat in the sauna. What a great place to get away from it all and relax!

Just because a guy goes to the gym regularly does not mean he's pumping iron and working hard to develop muscles. The same could be said of many a small group member. He's been asked to join a group and become a completely different person overnight, abandoning one set of values he's lived his entire life for another set he knows only intellectually. When church leaders assimilate consumer-members of the congregation into small groups, they form small groups that do nothing but consume.

It gets worse. Consumer small groups also take a toll on the leaders involved. The staff pastor over these small groups will always feel like a mother bird feeding helpless baby chicks in the nest with life support, commonly called curriculum. He or she will toil to keep each small group alive and each leader supported to prevent burnout, which usually produces stomach ulcers, not genuine growth. The lead pastor constantly demands that more groups be launched for the visitors who show up on Sunday morning.

It stinks to be a small group pastor in this kind of situation, and rightfully so. Being forced to expand a stagnant small group ministry carries its own stench.

It's equally unpleasant inside consumer-filled small groups. The members consider the small group pastor as a "gentle pest" who is constantly badgering them to edify, serve, and reach out. They know it's the right thing to do, but they're too busy with their individual lives to make the sacrifice. While mandates and pleas from staff members don't fall on deaf ears, people who have crippled themselves living out the world's values cannot walk out their faith when they hear this directive. They just feel guilty.

Tozer doesn't mince words on this issue:

> I think we are going to have to restudy this whole teaching
> of the place of the Holy Spirit in the Church, so the Body
> can operate again. If the life goes out of a man's body, he is
> said to be a corpse. He is what they call "the remains." It is
> sad, but humorously sad, that a strong, fine man with shin-
> ing eyes and vibrant voice, a living man, dies, and we say,
> "the remains" can be seen at a funeral home. All the remains
> of the man, and the least part about him, is what you can see
> there in the funeral home. The living man is gone. You have
> only the body. The body is "the remains."
>
> So it is in the Church of Christ. It is literally true that
> some churches are dead. The Holy Spirit has gone out of
> them and all you have left are "the remains." You have the
> potential of the church but you do not have the church, just
> as you have in a dead man the potential of a living man but
> you do not have a living man. He can't talk, he can't taste, he
> can't touch, he can't feel, he can't smell, he can't see, he can't
> hear—because he is dead! The soul has gone out of the man,
> and when the Holy Spirit is not present in the Church, you
> have to get along after the methods of business or politics or
> psychology or human effort.[1]

The smell of success overwhelms one's common senses

One lazy Saturday, a pastor took his time to walk through an
epicurean grocery store. As soon as he walked through the front door,
he was immediately drawn to the expansive coffee section. The smell
of freshly brewed coffee was stronger than a Klingon starship's

tractor beam. He simply had to taste that which produced such an intoxicating aroma. The smiling lady operating the sample table gave him a sample cup of gourmet coffee made from fancy Kona beans just delivered from Hawaii. After he took his first sip, he was a goner. The taste was as powerful as the smell; he had no choice but to grab the bag of beans and throw it in his basket without another thought.

After poking around the cheese section and repeatedly visiting another smiling lady giving away garlic-stuffed olives on a toothpick, he went to the checkout counter. That's when the reality of his buying decision hit him in the face ... or better stated, his wallet. He had indiscriminately tossed into his basket a one-pound bag of coffee beans valued at $29. However, he didn't have cash in the budget for this kind of purchase and would bounce a check if he bought the coffee. It was embarrassing, but he asked the cashier to remove the coffee from the bill and offered to bring it back to the smiling lady in the coffee section.

The smell of another church's success with small groups can also cloud one's mind. The dream of what his church could be motivates him to write a check that will surely be returned to him stamped "insufficient funds."

Larry Stockstill, Pastor of Bethany World Prayer Center in Baton Rouge, Louisiana, launched groups in 1993. He started 54 cell groups, whose mission was to reach unchurched people for Christ and assimilate visitors from the weekend services. Within six months, the 54 groups had multiplied into 108 groups, adding 600 new families to the church that year and bringing hundreds of baptisms of first-time converts.[2]

Word of this church's success with small groups spread like wildfire. Pastors from every corner of the nation flocked to Baton Rouge for this church's cell group conferences. I attended the first two events, savoring each minute of Stockstill's presentations. America finally had a model church where small groups were growing naturally with new Christians and members who hungered to lead new groups!

A few months after the first conference, I received disheartening phone calls from pastors I met in Baton Rouge. Each lamented that the small groups they launched after attending Bethany's conference were stagnant and unproductive. The leaders were burned out. The members showed up for meetings, but refused to share transparently. Between meetings, fellowship among the members was nonexistent. When I asked about outreach and relational evangelism, one pastor responded with cynical laughter. After a brief chuckle, he replied, "Our members are so nominal that if I don't laugh, I'll start crying ... again. I had no idea my church was dead until I launched cell groups."

These pastors did not realize—or were unwilling to admit—their churches were filled with dead members. After all, this reflects poorly on a pastor's ability to lead. Yet every pastor I spoke with desired to know why their groups were not growing like Bethany's groups. While their failure made common sense to me, they remained baffled.

In both conferences I attended, Stockstill was quite clear about how he began his first groups. In 1998, he wrote the following, which is nearly verbatim from what I heard him say at Bethany's conferences:

> I called together the group of 500 intercessors we had trained throughout the years and dubbed the "Gideon's Army." For years the "Gideon's Army" had been meeting every Saturday morning from 9:00 to 10:00 a.m. to pray for the pastors, church services, ministries, missionaries and the breaking of spiritual strongholds in Baton Rouge. I knew this group was

to be the "core" — anyone who would come on a Saturday morning to pray had to be open to the new direction the Holy Spirit was showing us!"[3]

In my estimation, thousands of churches have failed with small groups after learning about them at a mega church's cell group or small group conference. The model churches and their pastors are not at fault. At Bethany's events, Stockstill plainly described those he chose for the first groups and, most importantly, *why* he chose them. The blame for failure lies squarely on the shoulders of the visiting pastors who made wild assumptions about their churches' health.

A shiny apple with a rotten core

The most obvious of these pastors' inaccurate assumptions was that the members and leaders of their first groups—the "cream of the crop" in their churches—were fruitful Christians like the members of Gideon's Army. Some of the pastors I counseled stated they were stunned by the spiritual bankruptcy of their lay leaders, which was only discovered after months of hard work training them to lead new small groups. Looking back, they said they would have aborted their transition to small group-based ministry if they had known so many of their core talked a good talk on Sunday morning, but had no measurable level of spirituality the other six days of the week.

Traditional church life, with all its ingrown facilities-based programs, has produced believers who firmly believe that their Christian ideals are synonymous with their lived-out values. This is where many pastors go wrong. They assume they have a Gideon's Army, or at the very least, a handful of committed believers who are prayer warriors and soul winners as they form groups.

In 1999, I had an illuminating conversation with Pastor Stockstill.[4] When I asked about Gideon's Army, he said choosing these men and women to launch groups was obvious. These believers were far more committed to Christ and Bethany's mission than just praying for an hour on Saturday mornings. The people possessed a deep devotional life. Many committed an hour each day to prayer and were the church's core intercessors. As a whole, the members of Gideon's Army were constantly sharing their faith and reaching the lost for Christ *before* the groups were formed. Pastor Stockstill made his decision based on the current lifestyle and activities of a group of committed believers in his congregation.

Assuming one's church is healthy—or that a healthy core exists through idealistic discussions with leaders—guides a church down the primrose path to small group stagnation. Lay leaders and members may wax lyrical about how they love the Lord and ache to see the lost saved, but their words don't produce fruit. The proof is in their actions.

"If I build it, they will come"

Not all pastors are deceived by member's words, yet many still fail to create healthy small groups due to wishful thinking. They know their members have an excellent set of ideals and solid biblical training but lack the lifestyle of a healthy believer. The pastor envisions these members in action, creating his own field of dreams like Kevin Costner, who portrayed a farmer with a dream to transform a cornfield into a baseball field where all the great players would show up to play ball. In this scenario, the pastor's mindset is, "Once they get into a group and see what it's like, they'll rise to the occasion and live out what they know." The "if we build it, they will come" approach may assimilate large numbers of people into groups, but it rarely provides personal transformation and a new lifestyle for the members.

Small groups will not revive a dead church.
Dead churches need confession and repentance.

Churches with consumer-minded members must experience some God-given hardship to bring them to a point of confession. The members need to make drastic changes in their lifestyle, indicating repentance has taken place. When this has occurred, a new structure like small groups can be implemented successfully.

Solomon thought he was on the right path when he built the temple. However, God wanted more than a structure. He wanted intimacy with his people, and he demanded that they turn away from idolatry and worship him only:

> When Solomon had finished the temple of the Lord and the royal palace, and had succeeded in carrying out all he had in mind to do in the temple of the Lord and in his own palace, the Lord appeared to him at night and said: "I have heard your prayer and have chosen this place for myself as a temple for sacrifices."
>
> "When I shut up the heavens so that there is no rain, or command locusts to devour the land or send a plague among my people, if my people, who are called by my name, will humble themselves and pray and seek my face and turn from their wicked ways, then will I hear from heaven and will forgive their sin and will heal their land. Now my eyes will be open and my ears attentive to the prayers offered in this

place. I have chosen and consecrated this temple so that my Name may be there forever. My eyes and my heart will always be there."

"As for you, if you walk before me as David your father did, and do all I command, and observe my decrees and laws, I will establish your royal throne, as I covenanted with David your father when I said, 'You shall never fail to have a man to rule over Israel.' "

"But if you turn away and forsake the decrees and commands I have given you and go off to serve other gods and worship them, then I will uproot Israel from my land, which I have given them, and will reject this temple I have consecrated for my Name. I will make it a byword and an object of ridicule among all peoples. And though this temple is now so imposing, all who pass by will be appalled and say, 'Why has the Lord done such a thing to this land and to this temple?' People will answer, 'Because they have forsaken the Lord, the God of their fathers, who brought them out of Egypt, and have embraced other gods, worshiping and serving them—that is why he brought all this disaster on them.' " (2 Chronicles 7:11-22)

In this passage, God wedges a promise for Israel between two stern warnings. It's as if God is saying to Solomon, "Thanks for the temple. It's way cool and I'm glad to see you completed construction. You've thrown the full weight of your authority in the land behind making it a magnificent place for worship and sacrifices, but this isn't enough. I want you to put a greater amount of energy into bringing my people into a repentant lifestyle. Let them know that I'm as serious as a heart attack about this. If they don't stop worshipping their idols and start worshipping me fully, I'll turn this beautiful place into dust. If you don't want the world around you to point and laugh at Israel's disobedience, challenge my people to change their values and return to a God-centered lifestyle."

God stated all this to Solomon in a highly systematic way. Solomon must have been all ears when he heard the "When-If-Then-But" discourse. It left no wiggle room for interpretation.

Today's church is filled with consumer Christians who need the same stern warning. God's bottom line remains: "Set your new structures (small groups) aside to address the existing lifestyle of my people." By examining each part of the warning—or promise, depending on how you choose to view it—a pastor can easily see how to proceed with his flock. Here's a breakdown of each section, which reveals the step-by-step process:

"When I ... "

After a brief acknowledgement that God heard Solomon's prayers and accepted the temple for sacrifices, God reminded Solomon of the pestilence he inflicted on Egypt when Pharaoh showed his self-centeredness. His mere mention of plagues, introduced with the words "When I" indicates that he is planning to fight stubborn self-centeredness within Israel with the same intensity and fervor.

Consumer-driven members of dead churches need to know that the God of Solomon is the same God we serve today. It's plain to see that many Christians today worship their children, their possessions, their credit score, their careers, the home in which they live (or wish to live), and their personal dreams and ambitions more than God. God didn't like it when the Israelites put other things before him in

Solomon's day, and he's just as upset today! God will surely discipline the church that panders to a consumer mindset.

The first step toward correcting consumerism is to help self-centered Christians develop a healthy fear of the Lord. In Philippians 2:12, Paul urges the church in Phillipi to maintain a correct understanding of the Lord's position in the life of a Christian: *"Therefore, my beloved, as you have always obeyed, not as in my presence only, but now much more in my absence, work out your own salvation with fear and trembling"* (New King James Version). Commentator William Hendriksen renders fear and trembling as "reverence and awe; being afraid to offend God in any way."[5] Working out one's salvation with others in biblical community cannot be accomplished without a passionate desire to please God, which requires great sacrifice.

"If my people"

God begins his promise with a big "if" that seemingly grows bigger with each additional phrase in the promise. He's put the burden of responsibility on his people to do what is right. The dead church of today has two choices: Remain as a consumer-driven, watered down form of Christianity that has limited relationship with God and each other, or confess consumerism as an idolatrous offense to God, and repent by living completely differently to restore favor with God and his people.

"which are called by my name"

This powerful, yet often-overlooked phrase is typically viewed as a modifier for the first three words of this passage. One might think this is just a point of clarification. It is actually the first part of the process God requires of those with whom he intimately relates.

Regardless of all God had done for Israel and the beautiful temple, the Israelites still embraced old patterns of idol worship. These idols were considered a prize possession. By adding this phrase in the beginning of the promise, God required them to acknowledge they had taken God's name only, rejecting all lesser gods.

A pew-warming consumer may consider himself a Christian or a follower of Christ. Yet, he still loves his prized possessions more than the causes of Christ or the lifestyle of a true believer. So, the second step for a churched consumer is to confess the idolatrous nature of the world in which he lives, and then seek to think and live differently.

"shall humble themselves and pray"

Humility is the fruit of surrender. God desperately needed to see that the people of Israel had abandoned all thoughts of being self-sufficient or making sacrifices to false gods. Prayer to God Almighty alone was what he wanted. This would show the beginnings of a contrite heart.

The dead church must seek personal brokenness to find humility, where God is free to work in and through them. For pastors who have attempted to heal their churches through new programs, this must be surrendered as their own effort to create change. For individual members, they must permanently abandon the lifestyle of focusing on their own needs for what the Master desires.

When I was a little boy, I distinctly recall my father preaching a sermon called "Pierce my ear, O Lord." His text began with Romans 1:1, where Paul described himself as a bond slave. In this verse, he used the Greek word *doulos*, which is defined as a slave who has voluntarily given himself over to another for life, permanently relinquishing his rights to freedom. His *doulos* status was easily identified in public. He had given his life-master permission to pierce his ear with a nail, creating a scarred hole.

The piercing was permanently humbling for the slave, knowing he would never serve his own desires again. It was a burden for the master as well. By piercing the ear of another person, he agreed to protect and care for that person's needs for the rest of his or her life.

My father ended that sermon with a phrase he uses to this day: "It is the task of the servant to obey the master; it is the task of the master to supply the needs of the servant." This is the intensity of a relationship with God that brings revival to a dead church.

Confession vs. Repentance

Relational intimacy with God requires repentance. Sadly, many consumer Christians believe that confession and repentance are synonymous. I have often heard Christian brothers and sisters say, "I repented of that sin a while back, but I always seem to be going back to God for forgiveness in this area of my life." In reality, the person didn't repent of anything. They just felt remorse and confessed it as sin. Repentance requires adopting godly action to replace the sinful way of living.

Confessing sin takes a lot out of a person. Acknowledging the fact that one has sinned against God and then sharing that confession aloud to a brother or sister in Christ tops the list of spiritual achievements for a typical Christian consumer. No wonder no one wants to add the all-important repentance action to complete the process and show freedom from sin.

I must admit I am the chief of sinners in this area. Over a month ago, I blogged that I was overweight, stating I needed to watch my diet and begin a rigorous exercise regime. The confession was made just about as publicly as one could make it. I also created a personal reward for losing thirty pounds and keeping it off for three months, which I included in the same blog entry. The deal I made with myself was fun. If I lost my goal weight and kept it off for a season, I would then reward myself with an Apple iPhone. If I did not lose the weight, I would force myself to keep my old cell phone and not give in to my desire for a cool new gadget.

As I write these words, I weigh two pounds more than I did last month. Public confession and a very nice reward did not motivate me to eat less and exercise more in repentance. In fact, ever since I blogged about the deal I made with myself, I've done the exact opposite. My keyboard is orange from all the Cheetos I just inhaled.

If a doctor had diagnosed my condition as diabetes a month ago, I can say with some certainty that the goal of losing weight would have turned out very differently. In this scenario, the penalties of overeating far outweigh any reward (no pun intended): I could lose a foot or my eyesight to poor circulation. Now, that's motivation!

Herein lies the truth of the matter. Repentance does not follow confession when there is no fear of losing something of great value. Consumer Christians have all but lost their fear of God, and do not consider themselves bond slaves of Christ. They confess sin when things go bad in order to get back what they lost, not out of reverence for God or fear of losing everything and a communion with their Creator.

While it might seem appropriate to quote Kierkegaard here, a modern-day pollster's assessment of our society is far more germane. George Barna, who directed the study of religious beliefs and practices, has noted that the relationship between people's perception of their religious commitment and their reticence to make faith their top priority points to a significant disconnect:

Spirituality is in vogue in our society today. It is popular to claim to be part of a "faith community" or to have a spiritual commitment. But what do Americans mean when they claim to be "spiritual?" The recent Grammy awards were perhaps indicative of this breakdown between self-perception and reality. The members of the group that won the award for best song thanked God for the victory then immediately followed with profanities that had to be bleeped from the broadcast. It seems as if God is in, but living for God is not. Many Americans are living a dual life — one filled with good feelings about God and faith, corroborated by some simple religious practices, and another in which they believe they are in control of their own destiny and operate apart from Him.

The survey also noted that among those who say their faith has "greatly transformed" their life, just one out of four positioned their faith practices and pursuits as their highest life priority. It certainly seems that millions of Americans are fooling themselves into thinking that they have found the appropriate balance between God and lifestyle.[6]

Just 25 percent of those surveyed by Barna's organization said their faith practices and pursuits are their highest life priority. My guess is that the true percentage is even lower than one in four. Most people answer surveys by a standard of ideals, not using true values or real life practices. In 2004, I created a brief online survey for lead pastors. Among the questions posed, I asked, "Do your church members truly understand the difference between remorse and repentance as indicated by their lifestyle?" Sixty-seven percent of the pastors who answered the question stated, "No, my members don't really know the difference." Without a healthy fear of God, repentance will always be confused with remorse.

One might think there is no hope for a church filled with people who do not possess a healthy fear of God. I don't subscribe to this opinion. I firmly believe that God wants to transform consumers into spiritually productive members of the body of Christ. The challenge is how to lead church members into making this radical, 180-degree shift in values.

Spiritual zombies and the resurrection power of prayer

From the flood of calls I receive from pastors who can't figure out why their small groups are failing, it's apparent that a sizeable percentage of American churches are wholly or partially filled with consumer Christians. In *The Organic Church*, Neil Cole writes about a vision concerning the church:

> The vision was of a bride lying down on a couch, so weak she couldn't even sit up. She was so sick that she looked dead, but she was still animated, barely. It was as if she were being supernaturally kept alive against all the rules of the natural world, like something from a B movie about zombies. Her skin was pale green and practically falling from her face. Her gown was unraveling and gray with dust. Her hair was thinning and unkempt. But the amazing thing was that her face had a smile on it as though she were waiting to meet her groom at any moment.
>
> I didn't really need any interpretation. I just knew that this was a picture of the church in America today: sick, kept alive

by a supernatural force, but believing she was quite healthy and ready to meet Jesus.[7]

The first thing a pastor must come to grips with is the fact that he leads a church with some percentage of zombies (the walking dead). One would hope they would only be members on the periphery, but this may not be the case. These members may serve as deacons or elders, teach a Sunday School class, tithe regularly, and possibly serve as a small group leader. One can easily maintain status as a spiritual zombie in the subculture of the American church, traditional or contemporary.

Recognizing one has a problem is the first step in any change process. Therefore, a pastor must determine two things to see the zombies in his church resurrected from their stagnant spiritual condition.

1. *What percentage of the church membership are zombies?* Look past their involvement in current programs (especially small groups) and look at their lifestyle. Do they really pray? Do they spend time with unchurched people each week as friends? Would those unchurched people consider the members in question close friends? How much contact do they have with other members of the church or their small group between congregational and smaller gatherings? Are they living in accountability, growing spiritually, and hating sin with an increasing passion?

2. *Is the pastor himself a zombie?* He too must look in the mirror. If he possesses a lackluster prayer life, if he spends no time with unchurched people, and if he has no accountability for his actions and thoughts, then he has set the bar low for his leaders and members. A senior or lead pastor should not expect anyone to change

until he himself is actively modeling the lifestyle God wants for the active Christian.

The answers to these two questions will help form a point of origination. Without a clear assessment of where the pastor and his church membership lie in the zombie-"kingdom activist"[8] continuum, he cannot move forward toward health and vitality where small groups are required for continued growth.

What to do about it

God's stern warning to Solomon (2 Chronicles 7:11-22) is easily adapted to any church plagued with spiritual zombies. "If your zombies, who call themselves followers of Jesus Christ, will humble themselves and pray, God will forgive their sins and heal your church."

I won't school you on just how transformational prayer can change hearts and motivate Christians to sacrificially serve God. What you do need is a strategy to get people praying so this kind of transformation can take place. Let's get intensely practical. Here is one organized way to engage your church members to pray.

Prayer Groups *(for those who have yet to join a small group)*

Prayer groups are a practical way to give zombies an opportunity to find personal transformation. To ensure these groups remain a support system to the overall direction of a church's small-group-based ministry and not compete with it, they must maintain a short lifespan and without an appointed leader. Here's how they work:

At a glance
- Each session runs five to eight weeks.
- Eight to ten persons participate in each group.
- Groups meet for one hour per week in homes.
- Meetings begin and end promptly.
- Each weekly hour of prayer has six topics that are prayed through for ten minutes.
- Everyone prays aloud at the same time.
- The host moves the group from topic to topic at ten-minute intervals.
- A two-week break between prayer group sessions provides time for new groups to form.
- To help create new friendships, no more than one family or two individuals from the first prayer group should be in subsequent prayer groups (if possible).

Goals
- Increases the level of prayer for each individual.
- Encourages church members to open their homes to others.
- Provides personal transformation through the power of prayer.
- Prepares church members for the active pursuit of ministry with others in a small group.

Duration: One hour per week commitment.

Prayer groups should run for no more than eight weeks to keep the commitment viable. Some churches have experimented with four weeks and others six depending on the willingness of the church members. The consensus is that for personal transformation to take place, the prayer group must be sustained for at least five weeks.

In addition, praying for one hour per week with others is more than enough time for an individual to experience a radical new understanding of his or her spiritual purpose in life.

Everyone leads, yet no one is the leader.

The person who is hosting the group in his or her home facilitates. Facilitating is not difficult, and requires little or no preparation beyond picking up in the room where the prayer group will meet. Handing out the prayer sheets that the church supplies and announcing that it's time to move from one area to another is all that is required during the prayer group time itself.

Everyone prays aloud simultaneously.

While it may be odd to your church members to pray aloud simultaneously in their native tongue, this is the norm for corporate prayer in most other countries.[9] Participants are encouraged to ignore others around them and pray in first person whenever possible. Of course, if an individual prays too loudly, a simple tap on the shoulder will help him remember to pray with less volume. The wonderful thing about "concert prayer" is that it eliminates the ability for individuals to dominate the prayer time or remain silent.

Expand the groups by mixing it up.

Prayer groups should be encouraged to re-form after a two-week break and repeat the five to eight weekly prayer group meetings. The strategy behind this is twofold. First, a couple of weeks without prayer creates a relational and corporate prayer vacuum. This break will increase the desire to re-engage in a new prayer group, even if it means inviting new friends into one's home. Second, the break and re-forming of new groups keeps the individuals involved from becoming exclusive in relationship.

Re-formed groups remain fresh when the original prayer group members are in new homes with new people. If there is a flood of new interest as the first round of groups is completed, this will not be a problem if the participants understand that increased involvement is a primary goal. If there is little interest, existing prayer group participants simply sign up to pray with a different group of people. With either outcome, existing prayer group participants must help build participation by inviting at least one other family unit to join their second prayer group experience.

During the break

Between prayer group sessions, new prayer topics can be created from suggestions offered by first-round participants. The break also gives the prayer group implementation team (described below in tips for success) the time they need to assess the general health of the congregation through the first cycle. Finally, the two-week break gives volunteers time to rest.

How a prayer group looks in action

Bob and Susan are hosting a prayer group this week, so they pick up their copies of the prayer schedule at the back of the auditorium at the prayer group table. Before they leave, they look over the content and visit with the table worker to clarify anything that they don't understand.

Before the meeting begins, Bob and Susan clean the room where they will be meeting and find extra pillows so folks can kneel comfortably. Since this group only meets for an hour and does not begin with refreshments, a pitcher of water and disposable cups are placed on the coffee table in the room where they meet.

Everyone in this prayer group is aware that prayer begins at 6 p.m. and ends promptly at 7 p.m., so most of the people arrive a few minutes early. Just before they begin, Bob puts a note on the front door indicating that prayer has begun and to simply slip in, grab a prayer schedule, find a place to pray, and start praying. Susan watches for people who arrive late and points to the section where they are currently praying and returns to her time of prayer.

Every ten minutes, the topic of prayer changes. Bob or Susan informs the group when it's time to move to the next topic, which they read to the group. There's always a brief time of silence, but Bob and Susan start praying aloud right away and this gives everyone permission to begin praying aloud too.

The six areas of prayer tonight are different from previous topics, but always follow the same pattern of moving from macro to micro. Tonight, the group begins with prayers of thanksgiving for various aspects of God's character, which are listed on the prayer schedule. Next, the group prays for government officials in Washington, D.C., specifically asking God to grant them supernatural wisdom in their decision making. Then, the group prays for one of the church's staff members, spouse, and children by name. This is followed by each person praying for his or her own spouse, children, and parents. Next, the members are challenged to pray for themselves in the area of tithing their time for kingdom pursuits. Finally, tonight the group is asked to devote the last ten minutes praying for lost and unchurched friends by name.

At 7 p.m., Bob thanks everyone for coming over to pray, and reviews where the prayer group will meet the next week. If anyone has experienced a breakthrough in prayer, they are encouraged to share a sentence or two and keep it brief.

Tips for success:
- Implement prayer groups with a short-term team from your church. Mobilize existing prayer warriors, a representative from the elder or deacon body, and a staff pastor. The senior pastor must also be a participating member of the team, although he does not have to facilitate team meetings. He serves as the vision caster and a troubleshooter for the team. Limit the team's size to no more than seven persons so decisions can be made and responsibility affixed. When the team gathers, they must decide the best time of year to launch prayer groups, what to cancel to make room for it, which topics should be prayed over, and so forth. In other words, the senior pastor should not tell the team how it's going to work. He must ask the team to create a plan of action to make it work well and participate in that process.
- Preach a series of sermons on the power of prayer to enhance participation. Prayer groups should begin during the series. By doing this, the pastor can personally share how it has changed his mindset and attitude about the prayer topics.
- During weekend services, interview those who have experienced personal breakthroughs. This will drive home the power of prayer.
- Don't start too many groups. It's a simple process to provide additional sign-up sheets for new groups, and this keeps the groups you initially formed full of participants, which creates momentum.
- Ensure those participating have a way to share how God is transforming them through prayer.
- Use a map to divide your town or city into geographic zones for group formation.

- Hold the prayer groups on the same night as your existing small groups (my reasoning for this suggestion is fleshed out below).
- Provide prayer schedules for each person in each group (see Appendix A for an example).
- Consider canceling Wednesday-night or Sunday-night services (if you still offer them). If people are substituting an existing church activity for a prayer group, they will not be able to use the lame excuse that they are too busy with church meetings to pray.
- Provide childcare or assist anyone needing childcare with help so they can participate.
- Teenagers should be encouraged to sign up for a group. When teens pray together for an hour a week, it radically transforms them and their parents!

Do prayer groups work?

When we pray, it gives God permission to transform us. So yes, prayer groups work for all who are willing to participate and be transformed by time with God. While some will balk at praying for "a whole hour," after the first session they'll sing a different tune. It's actually a lot of fun once you get started. You may even create prayer junkies by starting prayer groups. (This should only concern you if these folks don't want to do anything *except* pray.)

This strategy presents one other problem, best illustrated by a statement I heard years ago while visiting a psychologist. As we began our first session, he asked me, "How many psychologists does it take to change a light bulb?" Not waiting for a reply, he added, "Only one. But the bulb must want to change." And so it goes with your church members. If they are unwilling to pray, they cannot be transformed through prayer.

Existing small group participation

If you have small groups that are in reality home-based collections of spiritual zombies, they too should invest the first hour of their meetings to corporate prayer. To test the waters to see if your groups are alive or dead, challenge them to do this just once with a supplied prayer schedule with two-minute intervals instead of ten minute blocks. If the small group members rave about it, then you have learned a valuable way to help zombies find life within your small groups. If they complain or tell you they're not interested in doing more of it, they need a personal visit from the lead pastor. That's right, when the head honcho shows up and urges the members of a group to drop to their knees and pray with him for ten to fifteen minutes, it makes a strong statement.

I know this suggestion sounds radical and very time-consuming. However, radical times call for radical measures. And before you ask, the answer is *yes*. The lead pastor should make a visit to as many small groups as is humanly possible to tell them how concerned he is about their lack of desire to pray and connect with their Creator.

Small Group Assimilation

As consumers begin to pray and God moves in their hearts and lives, they'll need a spiritual family in which to grow. Those who "graduate" from a two-cycle prayer-group experience will readily visit an existing small group and probably join that group if that small group is filled with kingdom activists who love to pray.

If you like the idea of prayer groups and you believe these kinds of groups will wake the dead in your church, start thinking strategically about the future. If you haven't considered the ramifications of a successful prayer group strategy, it's time to stop and ponder the infrastructure required to retain the growth:

- Do we have enough healthy small groups into which we can assimilate prayer group graduates?
- Are our existing groups small enough (under ten members) to welcome new families or couples?
- Do we have enough trained apprentice leaders in groups to give us the ability to multiply groups if they are flooded with prayer group graduates?
- Do we have a discipleship path for small group members set in place so new members can begin the journey into discipleship?

The best way to ensure that every question is answered fully is to gather a team and list the potential growth issues you will face. Prayer groups should never be embarked upon with one person making all the decisions.

Plan for success by scheduling small group leader training

If prayer groups produce transformed lives in the first and second cycles, it will create a pool of potential small group members. These kingdom activists will be interested in small groups now and can be assimilated into existing groups. Of course, this assumes that the small groups into which they are being assimilated participated in the hour of prayer each week and the groups have room for new members. Consider and plan for a positive outcome. Begin today by relating to committed small group members who have the potential to lead tomorrow, helping them see what lies ahead in ministry. (More on this in Chapter 5.)

If your small groups didn't follow through by incorporating intensive prayer into their meetings, do not attempt to move praying congregational members into non-praying small groups. It will undo all the hard work they have done on their knees. Focus on starting new, healthy small groups with them. (What you'll read in Chapter 3 will be very helpful in this area.)

Are prayer groups the only way to transform zombies?

There are probably numerous ways to wake the spiritually dead. I'm offering one way to help your church members find transformation, hoping it will spark something within your church. If you do what you've always done, you'll get what you've always gotten. It just might be time to attempt something different to stir things up. What can you lose by forming groups to see who's interested?

I fully expect some pastors—especially the creative ones—will possess ideas for a better change agent that makes prayer groups appear sophomoric. If you think prayer groups have no merit, then get busy in whatever way you can to bring the dead parts of your congregation back to life. Just remember that forming small groups for zombies does not transform them into kingdom activists. That's something that comes directly from the throne of God through the suffering of Christ.

The reason I suggest prayer groups is obvious. Prayer in homes will test your church to see if the members are healthy and sacrificial in their faith. If a sizable percentage of your congregation completes one six-to-eight-week prayer group cycle, it's a good indication that your church is not dead and your small groups (if you have them) just don't pray enough.

If you assemble a team that prioritizes and implements a prayer group strategy and find that no one in your church body is interested, then you've just discovered something important about your church.

It's dead. That's a hard pill to swallow, but it sure is good to know the truth. Living churches are filled with people who value time with God.

One last thought as you weigh the pros and cons of prayer groups: praying in small groups in homes is good. Praying for guidance on specific issues, people, and your church's mission is good. Prayer transforms people into the likeness of Christ, and that's good too. I take it back. There are no cons to prayer groups. Never mind.

The heart of the house is alive!

When a church is brimming with kingdom activists, naturally expanding life will be evident. People find personal transformation in the form of being set free from spiritual bondage. Physical and emotional healing becomes commonplace. Sins are confessed, the roots of sin are exposed and deep healing takes place. When these things happen, the kingdom activists cannot contain their joy over their newfound spiritual freedom and direction. This produces conversion growth and baptisms. This kind of growth is natural and personal for the members.

It is within this organically growing environment that small groups thrive and are welcomed by the church body. They give the healthy members a place to minister, be ministered to, and relate to lost persons in a transformational way. New leaders move into the position because it's the next thing to do, not a huge sacrifice.

It bears repeating: small groups will never bring revival to a church or raise the spiritually dead in a congregation. They will, however, allow healthy kingdom activists to do far more than they could do on their own.

Work hard to raise the dead through prayer before you ask them to serve as "home missionaries" in your small group ministry.   ◆

A note to pastors of vibrant, healthy churches
Is your church filled with members who are passionate about Jesus as evidenced by a sacrificial prayer life? Do your members love one another to the point of sacrifice? Do they reach friends, coworkers, and neighbors for Jesus all the time? Great! These members are not only ready for holistic small groups, but are probably anxious to live in biblical community and harness its power to do even more with and for God. Launching holistic small groups to expand the harvest you are now experiencing is going to be fun! This will give you and your church a great deal of forward momentum into missional living and missional church life. Please do yourself a favor, though. Read the rest of this book and do not launch a bunch of groups and hope for the best.

Many healthy and very alive churches have launched small groups and failed miserably. Quite foolishly, the pastors did the right thing at the wrong time; the right thing at the right time with the wrong people; or the right thing at the right time for the wrong reasons.

That's why the next chapter is such an important read. If you don't do the *right* thing with the *right* people at the *right* time for the *right* reasons, your small groups are not going to grow naturally.

The naked truth about lead pastors: attitudes and strategies that bastardize the nature of holistic small groups

In many churches, the lead pastor uses small groups to support the larger corporate gathering. Or, he views small groups as one option among many for church involvement. In either case, his attitude works against self-sustaining organic growth through the small groups. To better understand how these approaches destroy the holistic nature and erode the health of a small group ministry, let's explore two popular ways small groups are used today.

Small groups: a support structure for something bigger

Small groups are an integral part of many pulpit-centered church-growth strategies. At a small group conference I attended last year, I heard a well-known pastor characterize the small groups in his church as being "the grain elevators that hold the harvest from our creative and inspiring weekend services."

For this pastor, small groups are used as little collection cups for what he and a handful of others do on Sundays. The missional thrust for his church is the weekend event and he's at the center of it. The small group ministry is in place to support the main event, providing the visitors with genuine relationships, which are missing in the large services.

My father termed this strategy the "celestial funnel"[1] approach: move visitors from big impersonal events (weekend services) into an intimate environment (small groups) to keep them from leaving.

This model of attraction/retention is only effective at closing the back door if visitors join a small group and that group becomes more than a church meeting. Should a pastor and his staff leap over both of these sizable hurdles repeatedly, the number of groups swell to an impressive number.

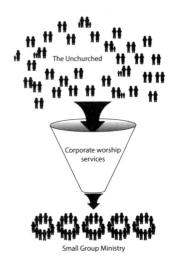

Although the model retains visitors, it has not-so-hidden drawbacks and negatively impacts the small group ministry. Rapidly increasing the small group population through a non-relational strategy erodes the values upon which holistic small groups are built. As you will soon see, the pastor who takes the bull by the horns and grows the church from his pulpit adversely affects the mission and environment for all levels of small group membership and leadership.

Relational evangelism

Some who use the funnel model argue that the small group members first bring friends to the services, but this is not the kind of "relational" evangelism needed. What is quickly forgotten by using this model is the personal process of evangelism: relate to unchurched people between church meetings, introduce them to other genuine believers in one's small group, include them in relational activities of the group to build deep friendships, bring them into the group, and finally, bring them to the cross and a place of commitment to Christ. (More on this in Chapter 4.)

In each church I've monitored that uses the funnel model, the small group members become lazy in the area of building relationships with the unchurched. As I have interviewed individual members and group leaders concerning their plans and success with relational outreach, my observation has been validated. They comment, "Who has time for relationship-building when another new family will join our group every few weeks? It's all we can do to absorb the visitors to make them feel welcome." Statements like this show a satiated desire to personally reach out and help unchurched friends discover Christ within a biblical community.

Once again, some pastors might argue that it's not a bad growth plan, just different than what other churches do. But this distinction lacks merit. When a believer reaches a dearly loved friend for Christ through a relationship, his own life is personally transformed as well. Additionally, because he was instrumental in reaching his friend, his level of commitment to disciple the new believer is far greater.

If a lead pastor desires to produce an evangelistically energetic small group ministry, he should stop flooding his church's groups with visitors from the weekend services and throw away the funnel!

Leader Development

Leader quality suffers whenever a small group ministry requires more leaders than can be organically "grown" in healthy biblical community. In the funnel model, new leaders must be appointed, trained, and deployed yesterday to keep up with demand.

Urgency + Leader development = Weak leaders

The urgency for new group leaders in this model forces many churches to use weekend crash courses, launching a range of new groups overnight. At best, these new leaders are given five to ten hours of cognitive training and then expected to lead. The faulty thinking is, "Develop people relationally the way Jesus did, shaping their character? That's not gonna happen. This church needs ten new group leaders by the end of the month."

Of the many concerns I have for the hasty selection and training required by this model, two rise to the surface:

Moral integrity—If a church is forced to move members into leadership rapidly, secret sin will remain a secret … for a season. When a leader must be removed because the person has been unfaithful to his or her spouse, everyone suffers the loss. Moral failure is common in churches that have weak or rapid leader training, so this is a concern regardless of any model your church might employ. The funnel model in particular ensures a small percentage of moral failure due to the number of new groups that must be rapidly formed.

Reliability—Can a person that has little to no relationship with a staff member be trusted to lead a group? Will the person be loyal to the Lord, the church's mission, and the leadership of the church? Appearances are often deceiving. When the pressure's on to roll out stress-inducing numbers of new groups before the next sermon series begins, unreliable leaders may be inadvertently chosen for the role.

Leader Support (Coaching)

Through statistical research and analysis, Dr. Jim Egli found that the practical, proactive coaching of small group leaders does more than anything else in a church's small group system to promote small group health and growth.[2] In an environment where leaders must be rapidly trained and deployed due to an outside source of numeric growth, the ratio between leaders and coaches will quickly increase, thus creating a non-relational and ineffective support structure. In other words, when a coach has eight or more groups under his or her care, the most a group leader will probably receive is a phone call once a quarter. This is not coaching.

Additionally, a group or leader in crisis will not receive necessary attention. Instead of helping the leader solve the problem before it reaches a crisis level, the coach finds out about a crisis situation after the fact and is forced to minimize collateral damage.

The funnel model wreaks havoc on leader care. It cripples the coach's ability to anticipate problems in a group or with a leader and take action before calamity strikes. There's too much externally fueled, non-relational growth to support leaders and groups the right way.

Member Intimacy

Vulnerability among group members takes a nosedive any time new people join a group. Even when the new member is known beforehand through other social contacts, some will struggle to share deep things. Previous relationships with the new member typically carries the group back into intimacy because they are fulfilling a relational mission. When a total stranger shows up to a small group gathering, however, members struggle to share deeply for a far longer period of time. No relational ministry or spiritual teamwork was involved to bring that person to the group.

I've led groups in which complete strangers showed up. Someone at the church told them where and when we were meeting, failing to let me know so I could visit with them before they arrived. During the meeting, I could have asked my group to share five non-threatening icebreaker questions and it wouldn't have helped anyone to speak openly. Fortunately, I took steps to ensure this never happened again, and my group bounced back quickly. Total strangers visiting our group with any frequency would have put a kibosh on deep sharing during meetings.

Some churches shield existing groups from this problem by forming all-new groups for incoming visitors in their funnel model. This fixes one problem, but creates a much larger one. A new group of strangers led by yet another stranger is an accident waiting to happen. One doesn't need a crystal ball to see burnout in this leader's future as well as member conflict in biblical proportions. When this group of strangers finally reveal their hidden agendas, expect a plague.

Staff Members

My heart goes out to the faithful staff pastors and assistants trapped in the funnel model. Their lives are consumed with making the next production a lasting success. They have no choice. They must launch numbers of new groups that, on a percentage basis, exceed some of the largest small-group-based churches in the world! Maintaining relational growth in existing small groups is difficult enough for a staff pastor. Who wants to work for someone who demands he or she must continually burn the candle at both ends?

Last year, I watched two of my friends—both excellent staff pastors in their own right—resign from churches whose pastors employ the funnel model. Both left because the lead pastor *stated* he wanted to see his church grow through members relating to the unchurched, but *acted* very differently with one 40-day adventure after another. These staff pastors were never able to maintain boundaries for family time or find an hour a week to go to the gym. Out of sheer exhaustion, they quit their jobs and left ministry altogether.

The Relational Way

As you can clearly see, I'm not a fan of the funnel model. It ensures the small groups will never operate as the church, only a program within it. In essence, the groups quickly become a cog in the lead pastor's clockwork.

Let me share one last concern about this model. The model doesn't call outsiders into a relational community through the relational community. Neil Cole makes a good point when he writes, "What we draw them with is what we draw them to."[3] Bring them in via a personality on stage, and they'll be most comfortable in a crowd watching that person in the future.

Herein lies one of the greatest strengths of holistic, small-group-based ministry: established relational connections. Seeking to expand the kingdom relationally creates a sustainable model for growth. It involves every small group member and becomes a way of life.

Organic growth prepares new leaders through discipleship, and retains visitors far more effectively. Why? New people find their spiritual connection to the church directly through relationships with believers in a small group, not from an on-stage personality.

What the funnel model reveals about a lead pastor

The issue at hand is not what's missing from the big corporate experience and how to provide it through small groups; it's the non-relational strategy the lead pastor has employed to build the church. How does he view small group ministry compared to his own pulpit ministry, to which he devotes sixteen hours or more per week?[4] How much time does he devote to equipping and releasing others for their ministry? Answers to these questions show a pastor's true set of ministry values. He invests the lion's share of his time where his priorities are placed.

Even the most committed pastors struggle with old paradigms of church growth. Recently, Joel Comiskey, a respected consultant and church planter, made this observation about a pastor he mentored:

> As I coached him over the months, I found that he naturally spent more time trying to attract people to the Sunday celebration service. He focused on sermon preparation, visiting, and dreaming of a crowd on Sunday. Cell ministry received leftover attention. When I challenged him on this, he acknowledged that he got a high from the Sunday crowd and didn't get that same excitement from cell ministry.[5]

The early church met in the temple courts regularly and the gatherings must have been sizable. The apostles probably shouted at the top of their lungs so everyone could hear. The gathering of the saints for instruction was vital then and equally important today. I just don't find Scripture to support the position that the apostles considered the house-to-house meetings as a sustaining support feature of the overarching temple court teaching.

To be fair, I believe many pastors embrace the celestial funnel model because they have failed to mobilize their small groups for relational evangelism. It's a result of growing impatient with consumer Christians. Taking matters into their own hands, they use the corporate gatherings to grow the church. The big, formal gathering is the part of the church structure where the lead pastor has a great deal of control. On Sunday, the lead pastor can—and usually will—direct what does and does not happen. In this area of control, he builds the church numerically with a personality-based strategy. Contrast this paradigm with Peter's challenge in his first epistle:

> I have a special concern for you church leaders. I know what it's like to be a leader, in on Christ's sufferings as well as the coming glory. Here's my concern: that you care for God's flock with all the diligence of a shepherd. Not because you have to, but because you want to please God. Not calculating what you can get out of it, but acting spontaneously. Not bossily telling others what to do, but tenderly showing them the way. (1 Peter 5:1-3, *The Message*)

When I read *The Message* translation of this verse, it drove the nail straight through the coffin lid on the pulpit-centered growth model. Leading a church into relational ministry requires taking the hard road of discipling and releasing others to expand the congregation. Just because it's hard or isn't instantly successful does not grant a pastor the permission to calculate what he can get out of it if he does it his own way.

Biting legs to herd the sheep

One of my favorite films is Babe. It's a movie about a piglet trained by a farmer to herd sheep in a contest held at a county fair. Babe tried to herd the sheep like a dog might do to please the farmer. No matter how loudly he shouted the word, "Woof!" the sheep wouldn't budge. So, he went to an experienced sheepdog for advice.

As you would imagine, the sheepdog said the way to move the sheep was to control the flock. He recommended biting a few legs to command their attention. The goal was to round up all the strays and herd the sheep into pens. (Sounds a lot like the mentality of the lead pastor who employs a celestial funnel model, doesn't it?)

Gently lead the flock

Babe discovered he did not possess the fearful bark and painful bite of a sheep dog. To succeed, Babe would have to abandon the mentality, attitude, and strategy of a dog for something more effective. When he related to the sheep and showed them respect, Babe and the sheep became a winning team. Babe learned there was only one way to win the contest: act like a shepherd and gently lead the sheep through the course.

Acting like a sheepdog didn't work for Babe and it doesn't work for pastors. God's design for the lead pastor is to gently lead others into biblical community. There's no room for control. One cannot drive people into groups and expect them to remain and be fruitful.

I hate to give away the ending to this cute movie if you haven't seen it, but I feel I must. It drives home the point about the kind of pastor an organically growing church requires. Babe quietly leads the sheep through the course, stunning the judges and the crowd. With precision unseen in any contest using a sheepdog, Babe wins the prize for the farmer!

The moral of Babe's story applies to leading a church of small groups: Make the depth of relationships your passionate goal in ministry and you will lead a congregation of small groups so large it cannot be easily counted.

The Cafeteria Plan: small groups are one option among many

Another prevailing paradigm among American pastors is the understated value and importance of basic biblical community (small groups) compared to other ministries. The pastor's mission is clear: get every person involved in something for the sake of retention. From the pulpit, he repeatedly makes announcements such as, "Plug into a ministry and get involved! Our children and youth areas need more workers ... our hospice ministry is making a real difference ... our small groups will help you feel like family and are a great way to connect. Or, you can join one of the teams that keep this church running so well. I know for a fact that we need a couple of accountants on the finance team."

Statements like this reek of desperation, which only piques the interest of the codependent. It also shows just how little the pastor understands about the power of biblical community and how it differs from support programs.

The Cafeteria Plan:
Teams, classes, ministries, and small groups are given the same priority.

| Visitation Ministry | Sunday School | Worship Team | Finance Committee | Hospice Ministry | Small Groups | Children's Ministry | Youth Ministry |

In the cafeteria plan, classes handle discipleship and teams perform the ministry and mission. That leaves small group involvement for those who primarily want or need fellowship: the lonely, bored, or parents who want free childcare and adult conversation. The pastor may desire the groups to be missional and holistic in nature, but they're rarely going to be more than a collection of people who have nothing better to do. A church's diffused missional thrust through numerous disconnected programs will never see growth through their small groups. Small groups don't grow when their only task is to connect members with one another.

Don't rock the boat!

The cafeteria plan is often found in churches where the senior leader is doing his best to keep the peace among existing program leaders and/or the old guard (deacons or elders). With a desire to implement something organic and missional (holistic small groups) without rocking the boat, he prioritizes small groups on the same level or even beneath existing programs of the church. This might appear to be a good initial strategy: get one's foot in the door so it can be opened wider later. Sadly, it just shoots the fledgling small groups in that same foot.

I learned this lesson the hard way in a denominational church where I led a group for five years. The young, innovative pastor introduced holistic small groups three years before we joined the church. It was quite evident that the church's growth from the small group ministry was the overwhelming factor that kept this dying church from closing its doors. I knew it, the pastor knew it, and every new member of the church knew it because they were reached for Christ relationally through the small groups.

The deacons, however, refused to give the holistic small groups the credit. They were unwilling to prioritize the small group ministry over existing programs because of the way groups were slyly added to the church's list of programs. These church leaders attributed the church's growth to the fact that the pastor was 30 years younger than the remnant congregation who hired him. Moreover, his preaching was far better than the guy he replaced. Their traditional paradigm was never challenged by the pastor's sneaky addition of small groups to the church's roster of dead programs.

During my years at the church, ministry tensions surfaced that were a constant source of frustration for the pastor. The Sunday school teachers said they felt like second-class citizens with all the interest in the small group ministry. So the pastor renamed the classes "facilities-based, curriculum-driven small groups" even though they were not holistic small groups in form or function. The stewardship team refused to reallocate resources away from dearly loved yet dead programs so the small group ministry could disciple new believers and train new leaders. (I considered holding a bake sale to raise money to purchase small group leader training resources. Sadly, I was asked not to; it would ruffle the feathers of a program's leader who used bake sales to raise donation money.) The team in charge of the church calendar allowed the chairperson of the women's ministry to schedule their annual brunch on the same day as a strategic planning time previously set aside for the members of all the groups.

When holistic small groups are not given priority over existing programs where the program directors have found much of their significance, a catfight results. When Etna and I left the church, we had the claw marks to prove it. Slipping holistic small groups into the church's cafeteria plan did not provide the transition the pastor imagined. Old time religion kicked biblical community's butt!

What the pastor failed to do was help the entire church leadership understand that holistic small groups are not just another supportive program. Unlike classes, teams, committees, or service ministries that perform a specific task for the congregation or community, holistic small group members gather regularly to focus on and experience the presence, power, and purposes of Christ in their midst. There's a night-and-day difference. Programs and teams *support* the church and provide outreach opportunities for those who are interested. The holistic small group *is* the church.

Dual purpose small groups

Some of the largest churches in America—churches that claim to be small-group-driven—operate with task groups that are challenged to "be the church" as well. I've queried senior and staff pastors of these churches about the reality of a dual mission. They firmly believe their meta-groups both perform a vital task for the church or a church service and live together in transformational, biblical community.

Yet if one takes the time to interview task group leaders and members as I have, it is painfully evident that the task is accomplished at the expense of seeking Christ in the midst. After all, the cars must get parked, the band must be tight for the first service, and the youth leaders must learn what they're teaching next week.

It's all about priorities. In task-oriented teams or ministries, the task cannot be put off or it will make someone look bad. The task must be accomplished. So, the task is often prioritized over focusing on Christ in the midst, regardless of what the group attempts to do with their time. Sure, member-to-member ministry happens, but for most task groups, it's accidental even when it's meant to be intentional! Because of this, a church must elevate holistic, Christ-centered and Christ-focused small groups over support teams.

Are teams bad?

I am not anti-team or bearish on programs. Weekend service support teams as well as administrative teams have their place and are important. A healthy level of volunteerism is a good thing for many practical tasks, but it's still volunteerism.[6]

Conversely, a church's holistic small group ministry is in a completely different league when one considers the underlying motivation. This familiar passage from Jesus' ministry speaks volumes in this regard:

> Now as they went on their way, he entered a certain village, where a woman named Martha welcomed him into her home. She had a sister named Mary, who sat at the Lord's feet and listened to what he was saying. But Martha was distracted by her many tasks; so she came to him and asked, "Lord, do you not care that my sister has left me to do all the work by myself? Tell her then to help me." But the Lord answered her, "Martha, Martha, you are worried and distracted by many things; there is need of only one thing. Mary has chosen the better part, which will not be taken away from her."
>
> (Luke 10:38-42, *New Revised Standard Version*)

Jesus separated the Martha stuff (getting things done through task groups, teams, and committees of volunteers) from the more important Mary stuff (focusing on Christ in one's midst in a holistic small group). This delineation must be clearly made in the heart of the pastor who currently encourages the cafeteria plan. For his church's small groups to become the missional thrust and grow organically, they must be elevated above volunteer-driven support programs and teams.[7]

This is not something he holds as an ideal. It must become a root value within his life and ministry to others. He must personally discover the presence, power, and purposes of Christ in the midst of a small group to change his perception. When this happens, he will never view the traditional programs and support teams as being equal to biblical communities of believers who prioritize Christ in their midst.

What to do about it

Are you thinking, "Has this guy been to my church?" Possibly. I visit numerous churches over the course of a calendar year. Even if we've never met, I do hope you will take what I've written personally. I mean it to be *very* personal. This chapter is all about a lead pastor's willingness to prioritize relational ministry above his pulpit and established programs, changing everything to achieve it if necessary.

Here's your first challenge: lead pastors must be highly relational if they desire to lead others out of volunteerism into relational ministry. Many typical pastors focus most of their time and energy on sermon prep and administration (the two job responsibilities that keep them employed). Even those who pride themselves on the quality of their relationships find themselves lacking as they move into a relational way of doing church through holistic small groups.

Maintaining and expanding genuine relationships

The pastor's survey I mentioned briefly in the first chapter was eye opening for those who completed it. It also provided revealing information about their lifestyle and ministry. The questionnaire was specifically designed to reveal strengths or weaknesses in regard to one's relationship with his Creator, family, church members, friends, and the unchurched. Here's a snapshot of the survey results, completed by 200 pastors of churches who stated they desired to "do church" through holistic small groups:[8]

84% indicated that they devoted *"a significant amount of time each week"* in discipleship-based relationships with others in their church. Of this group,
— just 30% reported they knew of their disciples' concerns, hurts, and dreams.
— only 49% reported they felt their disciples knew them intimately.

64% indicated that they felt there was an unhealthy imbalance between administrative duties and sermon-prep time compared to relating intimately to leaders.

62% indicated this statement was false: *"When I plan my week, I consider relational issues before I list administrative things I must do."*

62% of the pastors reported they prayed 45 minutes a day or less; 34% reported spending an hour a day in prayer; 4% reported spending 2 hours or more per day in prayer.
— When queried about intercession for their leaders with specific knowledge of how to pray for each individual, 10% of the pastors reported praying daily; 17% prayed 5-6 days a week; 19% prayed 3-4 days a week; and 17% prayed only 1-2 days a week for their leaders.

— The balance of the pastors 34% (a full third of the respondents) selected one of two statements instead of the choices reported above: *"I do not pray for the leaders I serve consistently, but I do pray for them on occasion"* or *"Truth be told, my prayers, when voiced, are surface level. I just don't know my leaders well enough to pray for their current, specific needs."*

40% of the pastors reported that they spent an hour or more with an unchurched person each week building a friendship; 42% stated they spent a couple of hours per month with an unchurched person; 18% (nearly one in five pastors) reported: *"I don't have an unchurched person who calls me his or her friend."*

[Mark Twain said there are three kinds of lies: lies; damned lies, and statistics. Twain was not wrong. Statistics are easily manipulated to support both sides of the same argument. I trust you to interpret this data in the most motivating way you can find.]

At the end of the survey, I asked each pastor to share a self-assessment of his personal ministry when considering his answers to the survey. A vast majority of the pastors wrote a variation of this statement:

"I must become far more relational in every aspect of my life to pastor effectively"

Here's the church, and here's the steeple

A friend who pastors a holistic-small-group-driven church took his daughter to a Mother's Day Out program at a nearby traditional church. A well-meaning adult taught the children to intertwine the fingers of both hands and recite a familiar children's rhyme you probably learned as a child. Knowing this was wrong, the four-year-old shouted, "No, no, no! The fingers are the church, not the building!"

As my friend told me that story, I could tell he was proud of his daughter, but he should have been proud of himself. Her rebuttal reflected her view of his values and lifestyle as a relational pastor. This little girl's daddy doesn't spend all his time at a church building. In fact, he spends very little time there. He invests most of his time with people in his home, their homes, and coffee shops.

If a lead pastor sincerely believes that the people are the church, that truth will prevail in his use of time during a typical workweek. Scott Boren, author of *The Relational Way*, wrote about Jesus' relational priorities compared to the average modern-day pastor:

Research on the Synoptic Gospels has provided estimates that Jesus spent about 50 percent of his time with 12 key leaders during his three years of ministry.[9] He did not ignore others outside of this group. In fact, there was a core group of about 70 who followed him. He also invested in these people, but with less of his time. And of course he ministered to the masses, as is illustrated in the feeding of the 5,000 and the 4,000, the Sermon on the Mount, and many healings. However, he prioritized his time, allowing him to give his best to the 12.

As I work with pastors in the church today, I ask them how they would break out the percentages among these three groups.

Consistently, they share how 75 percent of their time is invested in ministering to the crowd through preaching, preparation for preaching, counseling, and organizing mass events. The other 25 percent is divided among key leaders and the core group of the church. The time spent with key leaders and core group members is typically spent in getting stuff done for the crowd.

The modern pattern of pastoral leadership often results in feelings of usury on the part of key leaders. Pastors only have a small amount of time to meet with leaders to accomplish a task so that they can better minister to the crowd. That crowd is comprised of individualists who often will leave as soon as something does not suit their personal desires or meet their felt-needs. The pastor then spends most of his time and energy investing in people who don't have the ability or the desire to pass on to others what he has given them. His ministry stops with what he offers. He invests most of his ministry preaching to, counseling with, and organizing events for the crowd who cannot reproduce life in others.

At the same time, Jesus did not ignore the crowds. He ministered to them through miraculous signs and wonders that revealed the kingdom. While ministering to the masses, he was demonstrating the way of the kingdom to his key leaders. His investment in the 12 was not that of individualized discipleship. He equipped the 12 and taught them the way through his ministry to the core followers and the masses. Jesus had his eyes on developing a movement of people following the way, and he demonstrated this way, for all to see.[10]

How much time do you invest in your disciples
compared to preparing for a crowd?

I recommend that every lead pastor examine his use of time on a regular basis. If he reviews his last month's time use on an hour-by-hour basis and finds crowd control dominates his work week, it mandates change. Because weekend services occur every seven days, there will always be a pull to focus on building-based events instead of key leaders. For this reason, a pastor seeking to permanently change his time use must employ accountability with other pastors, his deacons, elders, or pastoral council. And not just one or two…all of them!

If you're confident you are people-centered and none of this applies to you, then confirm your opinion: complete the survey (found in Appendix B) after you have distributed copies to your spouse, children, and staff members. Invite them to answer the various parts of the survey on your behalf and sit down with you to discuss their answers. As you compare your assessment with their observations about your values, you may still find yourself in need of a ministry values overhaul.

Is anyone willing to run with the baton and hand it off?

To move out of a pulpit-centered or program-driven paradigm, a lead pastor must mandate change for himself while his church leaders simultaneously accept and live out their new missional role. It's the same as a relay race. The second runner must match the speed and direction of the first runner to successfully grab the baton and win the race.

Knowing you are probably feeling as low as a snake's belly right now after taking the relational survey, it's time I give you some good news: the relationally weak pastor is at a distinct advantage in his current situation. He can learn to crawl, walk, and then run with a few key leaders in his church and successfully pass the baton of ministry to them. Choosing key decision makers as running mates makes the process of prioritizing holistic small groups above other programs even easier.

Of one thing I am certain. You cannot use the same baton (training methods and traditional-program-implementation strategies) employed to win the traditional church race. It requires a completely different set of exercises and you can't run nearly as fast when others are training alongside you.

Pastors are definitely not from Venus

In 1992, relationship counselor John Gray wrote a best seller called, *Men Are from Mars, Women Are from Venus*. After reading his book, my take on it was clear: a husband thinks about enjoyable sex in the same way he would approach a hundred-yard dash. Reach the finish line as soon as possible. Conversely, a wife enjoys sex when it's preceded by quality, nonsexual time spent with the man who loves her. She also wants a sexual experience that would be characterized as a nice long walk through the park. So here's the million-dollar question: Would your church consider you more of a woman or man in regard to how you implement change in your church?

Last weekend I attended a wedding in which the minister (and father of the bride) shared a familiar passage from Ephesians 5. He briefly and gently challenged his daughter to submit to her new husband the way the church is to submit to Christ. Then, with a raised voice and a distinct change in tone, he turned to the groom and told him he was to "lay down his life for his new wife each and every day of their marriage without fail or compromise." He finished his rant with, "After all, Christ died for the church!" It was quite evident that the minister had left the building and the overly protective father was now officiating.

Please allow me to be blunt (again). Pastors have a nasty habit of implementing radical change the way an insensitive groom might act with his bride on their wedding night. Your goal is to be Christ to your church and die to the urgency to reach your ministry destination as soon as possible. In a radical lifestyle transition such as this, you must embrace the journey into relational ministry and focus on your own personal transformation first. This metamorphosis will yield a far better understanding of how your church can achieve more through holistic small groups compared to the programmatic approaches shared earlier in this chapter.

Following is a list of actions a pastor must take to effectively lead a relationally-driven church of holistic small groups.

Transforming action #1: admit you have a problem

If you've driven people into small groups the way a sheepdog would herd sheep into pens, confess it as a sin. Then, persuade your church leadership to let you pastor in a completely different way, ensuring you will delve into the ramifications of such a radical departure. I highly recommend studying Ephesians 4:11-16 with your elders or deacons to contrast what's been done in the past with what must be done in the future. Discussing Jesus' use of time developing disciples versus preparing for and being with a crowd is another excellent way to help them see what you've concluded about your current role in the church. You must help your leadership see that the issue is not with the pulpit itself, but the motivation driving the man who occupies it. That motivation is what must be dealt with and explored for what it will change for the church at large.

Or, you're the pastor who has diluted the transforming power of biblical community by making it one area of involvement among many through volunteerism. This too must be confessed and your church's cafeteria plan abandoned. Using the aforementioned example of Mary and Martha will help to persuade your deacons or elders to choose God's mission for his people over turf protection.

Working through either of these issues with your key leaders will not be easy or quickly achieved. Even if they initially agree in principle, they will soon see the depth of change required to prioritize and practice relational ministry, which may be met with opposition or even hostility. For this reason, you must relate to each of them individually in such a way that each knows your heart and is supportive before you call them together. If this is done, calling them together to search the Scripture for answers will be fruitful for dialoging about a go-forward strategy.

Transforming action #2: abandon the old way of doing church

The second step to pastoring differently is walking in repentance. This step does not call you to refine or improve the existing model, but discard it for something far better. In another excellent resource by Scott Boren entitled *How Do We Get There From Here?*, he highlights this often ignored stage of transition:

> The journey of repentance will lead a church to discover new ways to "be the church," new ways of participating with God in His Life. This kind of change impacts every aspect of a person's life. Transformation gets personal because it deals

with the personal beliefs, assumptions, and values that comprise a person's identity. The transformation journey seeks to change those things in order to line them up with Kingdom values. This journey has much in common with the journey Abram began in Genesis 12:1-4: "The Lord said to Abram, 'Leave your country, your people and your father's household and go to the land I will show you. ...So Abram left, as the Lord had told him." God did not call Abram to develop a better religion, or to transition religion by replacing the old with the new. He called Abram to a journey of life transformation, to repent of the ways that he knew in Ur. The journey of the church into small groups is no different.[11]

While this transformation is a personal identity shift as Boren states, the baton illustration mentioned earlier comes into play. You must help your church leaders make a repentant change of direction if you wish to personally walk in repentance. If you do not repent together, you're in for trouble. No one will be running alongside you to take the baton. They will still be focused on programs or non-relational methods.

In this relay race, you are the first runner that sets the pace, but you train for the race with a team. As you prepare for repentance in this second transforming action, keep two things in mind. The first is that you will hand the baton to your lay leaders as they experience transformation and they will in turn run hard in the new direction with key members with whom they relate. The second is that the race is won when transformed church members cross the finish line, baton in hand.

Transforming action #3: lead by example

Pastoring a relationship-driven church effectively will require you to live out new ministry ideals so they can become true values in your life. Quite often, pastors tell their leaders and members how important it is to be a vital part of a small group but they're too busy to participate in a group. Or, they're a part of a group but only show up for meetings. In other words, they do not take the time required to be a genuine friend to those in their group and their unchurched friends. They're living in the old value system of building-centered crowd control, challenging everyone to be the polar opposite. Your kids do what you do, not what you tell them to do, right? Church members and lay leaders are no different. If you don't prioritize face-to-face, transparent time with others, they won't either.

I know you don't have time to be more relational than you are today, so take a few steps toward the finish line. As you begin to do each one without thinking about it, you'll clearly see what you have to give up to keep doing what you're doing in relational ministry. Here are the first four steps:

1. Form or join a small group in which you are known and seek to know at least three to six of the members as genuine friends. Genuine friends are those with whom you exercise reciprocity (where you serve the person and he or she serves you). Real friends are in your home often enough to grab a drink out of your refrigerator without asking and you are in their homes often enough to do the same.[12]

2. Focus on group members in the six days and twenty-two hours between small group meetings. Pray for the members of the group by name each day and call them without a personal agenda. Don't ask them to do something for the church. Don't ask them to lead a

part of the small group meeting. Just call them to see how their day is going. After all, that's what real friends do (and busy pastors rarely seem to do).

3. Disciple someone in the group by spending an hour or two with him or her each week, but don't go through a discipleship book or do a Bible study. Spend time talking about life while your disciple helps you clean out your garage, you help him or her wax their car, or you both dig up flowerbeds for an elderly person on your street. Instead of telling someone how to be a Christian, show your disciple how it's done.

4. Help a small group member reach a long-time friend or a relative for Christ. You will experience personal transformation by returning to relational evangelism. The ongoing experience with this new convert will also show you what the new believer needs to mature in Christ within the context of a small group.

Transforming action #4: visit your existing small groups

After you've joined a group or relate to your existing group members as genuine friends outside the meeting, it's time to drop in on other groups to leverage what you're now doing. Although incredibly time-consuming, visiting groups is the most powerful thing you can do for your church and the small group ministry. I know this is hard to get your head around, but when you see what happens after the first two or three visits, you'll feel differently. As I shared in Chapter 1, you can't delegate this to someone on staff. It must be the senior or lead pastor for it to have the "wow" factor that makes an indelible impression.

The goal of the visit is to recast vision for a relational ministry among the members, asking them to join you in doing church in a completely different way.

Contact the leader

Call the leader a week in advance and share that you'll be visiting the group. Assure the person he or she is doing a great job, and you want to drop in for thirty minutes during the meeting. Ask the leader to plan for a time of worship, and leave the remaining time after you leave the meeting for dialog and a time of prayer. Inform the leader that you will arrive during worship and leave before the meeting is over because you've got a number of groups to visit and you want it to be a surprise for the members.

If asked for specifics, tell your leaders you want to encourage their members to participate fully in meetings, deepen relationships with other members outside of the meetings, and overlap their lives as a group with unchurched people.

One last thing: ask the leader to reserve an open chair for you on the other side of the room from him or her. This way, you won't create a spontaneous musical chairs game when you arrive. Tell him you'll slip in the front door unannounced.

Dress for success

Do people wear jeans and T-shirts to group? So should you. How about shorts and flip-flops? Shed your socks. It is imperative that group members view you as an ordinary person who serves an extraordinary God. Show your humanity by shedding the hired-holy-man image if you wear a collar or coat and tie on Sunday.

Show up late and leave early

Arriving ten minutes into the group's worship time will disrupt the meeting dynamics and change the tone of the meeting, but it makes for a greater impact. Leaving after you share is not a problem either. Inform the group that you're visiting a number of groups (if you truly are!) and you are unable to stay the rest of the evening.

Of course, if you disagree and feel it would be best to arrive early and participate in the entire evening, knock yourself out. If a whole evening per group wears on you or you don't think you can sustain that kind of time investment, you may wish to try what I'm suggesting and vary it to meet the needs of your small group members and leaders.

Share from your heart

After worship concludes, thank the leader for allowing you to visit the group and talk for a few minutes. Then share about the personal transformation you have experienced in your own small group. Explain that it came about because you chose to make the other members of the group true friends, and that small group isn't so much about showing up to a church meeting as it is overlapping your life with other believers and unchurched people. Clarify that God has led each person to the group for a special reason, and that the group must discover its purpose for being together and live it out. Every small group has a ministry and a mission. Challenge the group to refine both of these values by discussing what each will look like when the group is accomplishing them.

Show humility

If you've turned away from the celestial funnel or cafeteria plan mentality, this would be a good time to tell that to the group in the way of a confession. Apologize for seeing small groups as supportive of something more important. Then ask them if they can forgive you for doing this and walk in repentance with you to be a completely different kind of church, small group, church member, and Christian. This may be the hardest thing you've ever done, but it will build public accountability for you so that going back to Egypt is much harder to do.

Before you walk out the door, let them know you pray for them often (again, if you really do!) and you are willing and ready to help them be the church, not attend it. Showing up to a small group in progress will be something the members of the group talk about all week. However, if the last thing you tell them is that it's a privilege to be their pastor and how honored you feel to lead them in ministry, they'll talk about your visit for months.

Visiting all your groups could take a couple of years if you pastor a larger church. Frankly, I cannot think of a better use of time for a mega church pastor whose small groups are opt-in fellowship groups. It may be just the thing that motivates the members of a group to seize the ministry and missions opportunities all around them. Visiting hundreds of groups to confess that you've been doing church wrong for a long time will also keep you on a sober path of relational ministry yourself.

Focus on the environment where godly values are adopted

Preaching is a great model for sharing knowledge, but it rarely brings about transformation in and of itself. Our values are shaped through transparent sharing and living in community with other believers. A lead pastor must focus his time and energy on living in community. In 1990, my father wrote a widely read guidebook that challenged pastors to think "home" instead of "church building" as the epicenter of personal transformation:

There is a very important reason for the early church to be shaped in homes. It is in this location that values are shared. It may be possible to transmit information in a neutral building, but few values are implanted there. Value systems are ingrained through living together in a household. Something stirs deep within when life is shared between the young and the old, the strong and the weak, the wise and the foolish. In the house groups, all participated and all were impacted by the values of the others as Christ lived within them.[13]

Pastor, let this truth sink deep within you. Prioritize your small group ministry above your pulpit and your programs. Work overtime with your deacons, elders, or other decision-makers to move the missional thrust of your church into your small groups. Your Creator is counting on you to equip and release your members for their ministry through relationships! ◆

A note to highly relational pastors

Did you "amen!" your way through this chapter knowing you're not a sheepdog? Great! Do you use your time like Jesus did? Impressive! Do you, your leaders, and your church members view your small groups as the missional thrust of your church? Excellent!

Hmmm. There must be some *other* reason that your small group ministry isn't growing then. You better keep reading. I'm sure you'll stumble on the one or two things that are keeping your small groups from enjoying organic growth.

The naked truth about implementation strategies: common mistakes that promote lethargy and small group closure

Many pastors are perplexed as to why their small groups are not healthy after they launch groups (or additional groups). They also ponder why they must ride their group leaders and members hard to get them to do anything beyond basic attendance.

The root problem is the method used to launch groups. Typically, one of two pathways into small group ministry is taken. Both follow logic that has been employed to launch church programs for decades:

Strategy 1:

A. Research various small group models by reading books, visiting churches, attending mega church conferences, and interacting with other pastors in one's network or denomination.

B. Choose a model that has the best chance for survival or has the most upside potential for growth or assimilation into the current range of programs.

C. Cast a vision for groups with the elders, deacons, and other church leaders.

D. Recruit potential leaders from the aforementioned groups.

E. Train leaders over the summer months with materials recommended by other pastors or found on the Internet (usually six or eight cognitive sessions on various aspects of meeting facilitation, listening skills, and so forth).

F. Plan for a September "roll out" to start groups.

G. Count the number of people who made it through the training and start the same number of groups in September. (Twelve leaders equals twelve groups.)

H. Make pulpit announcements and set up an information booth for folks in the church to visit to learn more and find a leader they know and trust.

I. Supply leaders with curriculum and launch groups.

Strategy 2:

A. Cast a vision for a church-wide campaign with the elders, deacons, and other church leaders.

B. Buy a 40-day campaign kit and follow the instructions to the best of one's ability.

C. Advertise the church-wide campaign inside and outside the church building.

D. Contact members who will most likely agree to host a group.

E. Brief hosts on qualifications of the role (vacuum carpet and learn how to use one's DVD player).[1]

F. Form groups on Sunday, Day 1 of the "40 days of _____" (fill in the blank with one of a dozen campaigns designed by mega churches).

G. Supply hosts with curriculum if they wish to continue meeting after six weeks.

Much like a bucking bronco, both strategies produce groups who come out of the chute kicking up clouds of dust. The crowd cheers wildly and it's quite a spectacle! However, it's all over quickly. The bull tosses the rider off its back in a matter of seconds. Or, the bull runs out of steam, the rider hops off, and he walks back to the bullpen. For the church, the groups stagnate or dissolve and the pastor hides in the bullpen. Typical flowcharts for implementation look something like this:

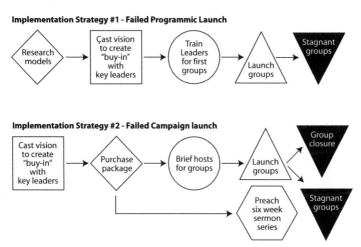

By now, you've read enough to know why these strategies don't create healthy, naturally growing small groups. To test yourself, review the flow charts above and note what is missing for launching a healthy, self-sustaining small group ministry. Better yet, find a clean sheet of paper and redraw a process of group implementation that would be more successful. (By completing this exercise, you'll engage the other side of your brain. Hopefully, you'll have an "aha!" moment about what you've done wrong in the past or what you were about to do oh-so-wrong in the future. At the end of this chapter, I've supplied a flowchart of how success has been achieved that you can use for comparison.)

Before you turn to the end of the chapter to see how well you did with your flowchart, let's explore the inaccurate assumptions, programmatic mistakes, and missing pieces in a typical implementation strategy.

Program-oriented implementation produces weak groups

If you create a small group implementation strategy the way you've launched other programs, you'll end up with a small group program. At best, it will be an organization run by volunteers (which was explored in the last chapter as being unproductive). A healthy small group ministry is a living organism that expands and multiplies from within. Therefore, a completely different way of thinking about and implementing small groups must be embraced to see vibrant, healthy groups a year or two down the road.

Develop your own model instead of copycatting others

Choosing a small group model before you have personally experienced success with holistic small groups is similar to buying a suit out of a catalog. It's a safe bet the jacket or trousers or both will not fit well, even if you ordered the right size. The suit may look great on the model posing for the photos, but your body type is completely different.

Contrast this with a custom-made suit. Your measurements are taken and fabrics are chosen. Then you visit the tailor again halfway through the process so he or she can ensure the suit is being made to fit you perfectly. Then there's a final fitting. On occasion, more alterations are made for the correct fit. If you gain a few pounds, the tailor lets out the trousers and sews in buttons for suspenders. If you lose a few pounds, the tailor can fix that too. A custom-made suit can be worn for years with minor modifications because it was designed especially for the man wearing it.

You will always feel a strong pull to adopt another church's model so you don't have to recreate the wheel. However, take into consideration the downsides:

• You may become so excited about the model that you cast a vision for the model and not the values that drive it. (This is very common; don't dismiss it as something you'd never do.)
• Forcing your church members and lay leaders to use someone else's model when they needed something completely different is highly counterproductive.

Here's the deal. You and your church are unique. Remain unique! Instead of being a cookie-cutter mega church wannabe, focus your time and energy to create a small group oversight and leader training that is a response to the growth and feedback from your first groups.

A successful implementation strategy is
as reactive as it is proactive

After your first groups are producing fruit, you will know how to alter the model or structure as often as needed so it is supportive. Learn what you can from churches with successful holistic small groups, but don't mimic them or expect their results just because you put on their suit. Develop your own way of discipling new believers, training members to lead, supporting groups, and organizing people into groups. By experimenting with different ways of structuring, managing, and organizing small groups to see what works at your church with your members, you'll create a model that fits you perfectly.

A model for oversight and training that you create along the way is far better than adopting another church's model that everyone struggles to embrace in a totally different environment.

Do not make congregational assimilation your primary goal

If your strategy is to get everyone into a group as soon as possible so they will minister to others, you're about to launch a static small group ministry. While congregational assimilation is indeed a goal, it must not be your first goal. In fact, it's not the second or even third goal. In the beginning, you will have far more important things to accomplish before enfolding the members of the church body into groups.

For the first few months to a year, you must focus on pilot groups to create a healthy pattern for the future. Next, you must focus on developing a discipleship pathway to maturity for small group members as you train your first group leaders. And finally, you must create some sort of "boot camp" experience for incoming church members to ensure they do not pollute your groups with consumerism. When these things are in place and operating, then you can slowly assimilate those in the congregation who are embracing the values that support holistic small group life.

Don't launch a bunch of groups until you can produce healthy groups

It's no fun to make mistakes, but it's how most folks learn. However, making the same mistake in ten different groups simultaneously is not only foolish, it may be disastrous. Launching a number of groups when you've never had experience launching one healthy group makes no sense. Implementing holistic small groups requires an experimental mindset and cautious forward movement.

As you have learned in the first chapters, holistic small group ministry is vastly different from church programs such as Sunday school, home Bible studies, or fellowship groups. Moving into groups too fast with inexperienced leaders and consumer-minded members is a characteristic of an impatient pastor.

Instead, create one pilot or prototype group. This experimental group will teach a handful of key people how to live and minister in a biblical community through shared experience. By prototyping, you will gain firsthand knowledge of your key leader's values and a better understanding of what lies ahead with the balance of the congregation.

As you make the shift from programs to organically growing small groups, you will make a lot of mistakes. Make them on a small number of people who love you dearly and possess a willingness to experiment with a completely new way of doing church. When you get it right, you will have a healthy pattern group for others to emulate.

Your existing leaders may not make the best small group leaders

Deacons, elders, Sunday school teachers, and program leaders are often the first people tapped for small group leadership. Many lay church leaders have no heart for people. Or they don't understand the difference between leading a group of people on mission and heading up a program or teaching a class. The theory behind holistic small groups is not hard to grasp. Living it out is quite different from traditional church life and many churches fail with small group ministry by ignoring this fact and placing the wrong people in leadership.

When a completely new way of doing church has been adopted in principle, every member, leader, and staff member must earn their position in the new model. In essence, all your heroes become zeros. Everyone starts over at the beginning to invest in others, allow people to serve them humbly, reach friends for Christ and disciple them, and so on. Your potential leaders should be trained to be healthy members before you select them as leadership candidates. Let them prove they can crawl before you ask them to sign up for a marathon. If they can't or won't be a solid group member, they are not ready for leadership.

Don't set a multiplication date for your prototype group

The naked truth about prototyping is that it's messy, time-consuming, and *not about training leaders*. Prototyping is about creating a functional, healthy pattern group to replicate. The prototype group members are gaining a great deal of leadership training by participation, but the goal is personal transformation. Their changed lives will fuel health in future groups and set the bar high for membership.

Pastors make a big mistake when they think, "We didn't achieve everything we hoped to accomplish in our four months together in the prototype, but the first groups will have the time to do far more. I'm sure they'll make us proud."

If you and the other members of your prototype group cannot develop a deep friendship by hanging out with one another outside of formal gatherings, you should not replicate this lack of community in future groups. If your prototype group has yet to reach two or more people for Christ and bring them into your group to successfully begin a discipleship process with them, do not launch more groups. You have not modeled relational evangelism for those who will serve as your first small group leaders. If your prototype group does not experience the presence, power, and purposes of Christ in a transforming and power-ful way week after week when you gather, it is not yet time to multiply your group. These issues indicate that your group is not mature or is not yet working well enough to be a healthy pattern group.

The failure to achieve the goals of a healthy small group prior to multiplying that prototype group is a recipe for future trouble. Small groups typically don't become stronger in future generations. They weaken when leaders and members form new groups and the bond with senior leadership is not as great as in the first groups. For this reason, you must—without excuse or exception—achieve everything you want groups to achieve five years from now in your prototype group *before* you send the members out to lead new groups. Get it right in the prototype phase or face the consequences!

Your leader training must be experiential

Most small group leadership training I've reviewed only delivers cognitive information. It supplies the person with knowledge of group life and leadership in a classroom setting. Few people learn solely through cognitive training methods. Most learn by doing, and gain confidence by doing something repeatedly. This is the kind of leadership training your group leaders will require, especially those that lead the first groups of people. (More on this in Chapter 5.)

Jesus developed unschooled, ordinary, working-class men into world-changing disciples by challenging them to walk with him and serve God. He did this because he knew they required downtime with him to process what they saw and learned earlier in the week.

The training you provide your first leaders must give them experience in actual ministry and missional settings from which to learn valuable lessons. Watching your members learn and grow will also aid you in choosing leaders who live out what they know. When experience has transformed a person into a minister with a mission and a ministry, you've developed a powerful small group leader.

What to do about it

Because a holistic small group ministry grows organically from within, it must be strategically implemented at a pace that maintains health and fruitful ministry. In the best-case scenario, this process feels pitifully slow to the lead pastor. Remember the children's story about the tortoise and the hare? When you are implementing groups the right way, I promise you'll not have one square inch of fur on your shell.

The believers who will populate your first groups must undergo a values shift away from consumerism and a building-centric mentality about church. Their mentality must move from volunteerism to seeing how holistic small group life enables them to live out their spiritual purposes in life. Those who lead your first groups must also understand the highly relational nature of group leadership. They must fully grasp that their group gathers regularly to focus on the presence, power, and purposes of Christ.

It's time to take out a clean sheet of paper and start over if either of the implementation strategies I've discussed thus far are what you have in mind or what you've already done (especially if you now have struggling groups).

What you will read in the balance of this chapter is a paraphrased overview of *How Do We Get There From Here?*, a resource I mentioned in Chapter 2. The author, Scott Boren, invested two years while on staff at TOUCH researching change theory and interviewing churches that failed to produce a healthy small group ministry (failure teaches far more than success). While I have both distilled and embroidered the content of his excellent process and broken down a few of the steps for clarification, you would do well to read this book as soon as possible. It will become a guiding light for your church's transition into a small-group-based expression of the body of Christ.

Step One: Determine your point of origination

I bought a GPS unit that provides turn-by-turn navigation when I'm driving to an unfamiliar destination. However, the gizmo is useless when it can't find a satellite to pinpoint my current position. You want the members of your church to live out their faith and be mission-driven. This is your destination. But do you know why they are not living it out today? What's holding them back? What have they yet to experience to become missional? This is your point of origination. If you don't determine where the members of your church are today with their spiritual walk and values, you will never implement holistic small groups with success.

Paul spoke to this when he wrote, *"For by the grace given me I say to every one of you: Do not think of yourself more highly than you ought, but rather think of yourself with sober judgment, in accordance with the measure of faith God has given you"* (Romans 12:3). Any pastor who desires to launch healthy small groups that reach the lost and experience powerful times together must make a sober judgment about a range of issues in his church. His own weaknesses in relational ministry must be examined carefully and corrected. He must also work with his staff members and lay leaders to help them determine where they are with God today. Finally, he must not ignore the first members of the first groups. They too must examine their point of origination to go anywhere. If all levels of small group oversight, leadership, and membership don't take stock of their current values, a church will be unable to chart a course and reach any destination.

Small group ministry is a player's game. There's a large field
in which to work as a team member, but no room for spectators

Gaining a firm grasp on the spiritual condition of your sheep will
not only help you start healthy small groups when the time is right,
but also help you determine the kind of discipleship path to take them
into spiritual maturity.

Another area in which you must employ "sober judgment" is how
well your church is living up to the vision or destination God has
given you for your church. If it's missing the mark, this can be excellent motivation to do something completely different to get better
results.

Find a handful of key leaders who comprise the core of your
church and pray with them to determine where you are today. Take
the relational survey found in Appendix B. Use church health tools
such as the survey offered by Natural Church Development.[2] Then
shore up the obvious weak areas in your church as part of your implementation strategy. By doing this, you will know what you must
do to prepare your church for life, ministry, and missions through
small biblical communities commonly known as small groups.

Step Two: Clarify God's vision for your church

A church's vision statement describes the kind of church they
know God wants them to be, which is their destination. Take a good
hard look at your church's vision statement with the core leadership
of your church. Does it accurately reflect the destination God has for
your church? If so, how are you doing on a scale of 1 to 10? Allow
everyone in the room to share a number and share—without
condemnation—why their score was so high or so low. Take the time

to dialog about how you're doing and what's missing. This won't be easy, but it's important.

If the average score is low and very concerning to your leaders, that's great! This will provide a strong sense of urgency to do something completely different by abandoning the old, programmatic ways that do not fulfill God's vision for your church.

If your church does not have a vision statement, you—along with your core leaders—must develop one as soon as possible. It will become your "true north" and a measuring stick for everything you do in ministry. Here's a piece of unsolicited advice: Craft a statement that is simple enough for a six-year-old to recite. People won't remember it if it's long or wordy.

When your church's core leadership concludes the only way to fulfill God's vision for their church is to do it through holistic small groups, it's far easier to make decisions about how to prepare various parts of the congregation for change and move into holistic small group life over the course of the next few years.

If your core leadership cannot agree that a shift away from programs and building-centered activities is the way to fulfill the vision, you should not launch small groups. They will not receive the priority they deserve to be healthy and productive.

You may be able to launch supportive groups that provide fellowship, discipleship, or Bible study for the members, but they will never be holistic in nature. Time requirements for the group leaders and members cannot be divided between the group's mission and ministry to one another and a plethora of other church activities and programs. Holistic small groups require the support, calendar space, and financial backing of the local church to sustain discipleship efforts and leadership training.

Your church leaders must *unanimously* come to a conclusion that the church's vision cannot be fulfilled without a purposeful, sacrificial shift away from building-centric programs. If you do not do this, it will come back and bite you repeatedly and you will not succeed with holistic small group ministry.

Step Three: Develop a small-group-driven mission statement with an implementation team and move forward together

A mission statement describes the *direction* and the *vehicle* the church will use to fulfill the vision (the destination). The mission should never be crafted and executed by one person because of the way it will dynamically change the way everyone "does church" through small groups instead of programs.

Inviting a team of leaders to craft a mission with small groups in mind also increases support and ownership. Here are some helpful tips concerning forming a team and being the kind of leader they need to shift mission and ministry in a church from programs to small group life:

• The lead pastor must facilitate the implementation team. Like Moses, he must remain the one who casts and recasts the vision. He must ensure the mission is clearly understood among the team and those who trust the team (the church body).

• A deacon or elder should represent this decision-making group. The best way to do this is to ask one or both of these groups to prayerfully appoint the right person to work on the team. When these groups meet in coming months, wise council will be offered to the representative and the elder or deacon will also explain what must occur for the directional shift to be successful.

• Key influencers in the church should be considered for team membership as well. They may represent a part of the church that the lead pastor does not influence.

• A "small group champion" must be chosen for the team. In small churches, the lead pastor fills this role as well until there is enough growth to bring a full-time person on to be the champion. In larger churches, a staff pastor fulfills this role.[3]

The ideal team is four to seven persons who commit to working on the missional direction of the church and who comprise the core of the first prototype group. This gives them firsthand experience with holistic small group life so they can accurately make decisions about the following:

• The general health of the church
• Existing obstacles to implementation
• The speed with which the first groups should be launched to maintain health (relational evangelism, mentor-based discipleship, experiential leader training, and true biblical community)
• The various components required for a solid discipleship path
• The personal objectives that must be met to extend small group leadership to a person
• A healthy ratio of groups per coach during the first stages of implementation
• Which programs must be scaled back to make room in the budget and calendar for equipping weekends, leader retreats, discipleship resources, and training events

I almost forgot! There are two additional and very important things you need to do as you implement step three:

• Determine a strategy to transition the work of various church ministries into the life of the small groups so these ministries support the small groups instead of compete with them.

• Rewrite the job descriptions of various staff pastors to include adequate support for small groups (especially the children's pastor).

Of one thing you can be certain: Too much is happening for one person to implement this church-wide shift alone. Pastor, don't try to do it by yourself!

Step Four: Review steps one and two with your staff and lay leadership

People forget why they're doing what they're doing after just a few weeks. At this point in your implementation process, it is imperative that you review what was discovered in the first two steps with your leadership before the team experiments with a prototype group. In fact, it should be brought back up for dialog to ensure it is still valid in the minds of each team member, the church staff, and your deacons or elders.

When you launch your first group, everything changes for the participants. Those involved will redefine "church" as you lead that group of people to reach friends for Christ and disciple them. For some, this will be akin to finding their lost tribe. In fact, people quickly abandon the old way as soon as the new way works, which causes problems. Much of the church has not transitioned to relational ministry and will need support for the next few years. If this happens, you must redirect the team to consider the needs of the traditional church and not abandon them.

Then there's the other side of the coin. Do not be surprised if leaders—people you *thought* you knew intimately—come to you and say, "I know this is what God wants us to do as a church, but I just can't commit to it." In so many words, you may hear they have no desire to be that transparent with other believers, they're unwilling to invest that much time into ministry, or they are unwilling to give up the program involvement in which they've been intrenched for many years.

This is always difficult for lead pastors in transition. They think they know their lay leaders, but they don't. The lay leaders think they know what they are ready to do for God, but it's just a lofty ideal. As a general rule of thumb, people cannot commit to anything new until they've actually tried it and found it to be a preferred method. What rings true to the ears isn't always easy to adopt as a new lifestyle.

By revisiting your point of origination and destination with your implementation team, elders, and deacons on a regular basis, you can alleviate some of the dropouts and conflict that will certainly arise.

Step Five: Develop healthy pattern groups by prototyping

In the early 1970s, Japanese carmakers imported automobiles to the U.S. In less than ten years, they ripped the automotive rug out from under domestic carmakers. This was not difficult. American cars were gas-guzzlers, undependable, and in some cases downright dangerous to drive (the Ford Pinto).

Why did the Japanese do so well with their ugly little econoboxes? *Dependability.* Compared to U.S. manufacturers, Japanese cars were "maintenance free." After all, they worked out all the problems with these models years earlier on the roads of Tokyo. The cars were brand new off the assembly line, but the technology was two to three years old.

To launch an organically expanding small group ministry, you *must* create pattern groups that are successful before you attempt to mass-produce them. With healthy, working prototype groups, you can prove to your lay leadership—and then your congregation—that your church's vision is being fulfilled successfully through holistic small groups. If you can produce one small group of Christians who have found personal transformation, are reaching friends for Christ, and are discipling the new believers successfully, you will have a little mound of success on which to stand.

What makes for a healthy prototype group?

While the values, components and results of a healthy small group are certainly something your implementation team must decide together, here are the basics of what you must achieve for basic health in your first group:

- Consistently enjoy an "Upper Room" experience with Christ during your gatherings, shedding your personal agendas for whatever Christ desires to do in your midst.
- Overlap your lives between meetings and become true friends.
- Help each other relate to and win friends for Christ.
- Bring those new Christians into the prototype group as the first new members.
- Begin a discipleship pathway toward spiritual maturity with the new believers.
- Create a high level of ownership for each member of the group as each person leads in ministry to one another in and outside the meetings.

Is prototyping holistic small groups really that easy?

All this sounds somewhat effortless in theory, but I know pastors of rapidly growing congregations who can't produce a small group that achieves these basic goals no matter how hard they try. They might have been able to do it twenty years ago when they were flat broke and still a relational church planter, but they're insulated from most everyone today.

The common problems discovered by pastors when prototyping are numerous:

- Many pastors do not spend enough time with friends "doing nothing" like hanging out, watching TV, going to the movies, or playing board games. Learning how to do this while prototyping can be very difficult because many pastors are workaholics and see this as an unproductive use of time.
- Some pastors don't have unchurched, non-Christian friends. Pastors may know an unchurched person who lives in the neighborhood as an acquaintance, but this person is not a genuine friend. This must be corrected to create a healthy DNA for future group leaders and members.
- Pastors love the sound of their own voice. They like to do all the talking, everyone in their group expects them to do all the talking, and the group members never gain a sense of ownership of the group or the freedom to share transparently. The only things pastors *don't* like to talk about are their personal struggles and confessing sin. Their inability or refusal to be vulnerable diminishes transparency in the prototype group.
- For many pastors, relationships with other believers are numerous and shallow. They don't relate to anyone in the church on a deep level because they're too busy. Or, they're fearful they'll be exposed for being a normal, sinful human saved by grace (which may have merit if they have a henchman in their midst).
- No one feels close enough to the lead pastor to speak into his life when he needs it.

Although it may be an uphill battle, the lead pastor must launch a prototype group that accomplishes everything he or she wants all the future groups in the church to achieve. Important components such as relational evangelism and discipleship cannot be implemented later. If it can't be achieved now with the lead pastor in charge of the group, others will not be able or willing to do it later.

How long is the prototype phase?

Most first-generation prototype groups take a full year to become mature enough to multiply. After all, the pastor must lead the prototype group in addition to leading his church. Prototyping requires double the effort during this phase of transition. A year may seem like a very long time, but it is actually the minimum amount of time required to invest in future leaders to shape values, bond with them, and become close friends with their unchurched neighbors, coworkers, and buddies. Jesus poured his last three years of life into his disciples, who turned the world upside down for God. Investing a year into your key leaders will reap benefits for decades.

Never rush the prototype phase. My high school English teacher had a sign on the wall of her classroom just above the clock, where the students were sure to see it. It said, "If you don't have time to do it right, where will you find the time to do it over?"

Why must I lead the first group?

Delegating leadership of the prototype group to a staff pastor may seem like the right thing to do, but I do not recommend it. To effectively lead others out of programs and into relational ministry, the lead pastor must show the way. Your staff, lay leaders, and church members must know you are as serious as a heart attack about transitioning away from programs and into a relationship-driven model.

One other important aspect of personally leading a prototype group must be explored. You will understand the implications of launching a holistic small group ministry far more if you are involved at the grass roots level. Without your leadership in the first group, you are a spectator. By delegating prototype group leadership, you will inadvertently sabotage growth in the first groups with an outsider's perspective.

If you are unwilling to lead the transition away from building-centric programs by prototyping the first group, it says a lot about you and what you truly believe. Is the priesthood of all believers just an ideal, or a lived-out value for you?

Do not expect to succeed with holistic small groups if you don't have the time, current relational capacity, or willingness to lead an experimental group to create a healthy pattern group. If you feel you are simply too busy to do it today, then you are not ready to launch a holistic small group ministry in your church. Work hard over the course of the next twelve months to change your workload so that you can pioneer the transition next year.

My first prototype group has achieved our goals. When can we branch out and assimilate more people into new groups?

It is at this very place that many pastors make a colossal mistake. The error is multiplying the first healthy, functioning group into four, five, or even six new groups. Doing this destroys the level of healthy biblical community residing within the initial group. Never forget there is strength in numbers. Growing in strength must remain your focus at all times.

When the members of your prototype have successfully facilitated meetings, led out in outreach events, ministered to other members of the group, and the group has seen conversion growth, you should multiply it into two groups. This may feel like a painfully slow way to expand your holistic small group ministry, but it is exponential growth. You just doubled the number of healthy small groups in your church. That, my friend, is something to brag about!

Moving from one prototype group to two will be far more challenging than you might imagine. The main reasons behind launching just one new group are:

• The people in the original prototype group have learned how to be functioning members, not leaders. They've watched you—the lead pastor—facilitate and lead the group in ministry and into its mission. You have skills and training they may not possess. It will not be easy to emulate the lead pastor when he's no longer in the room.

• Launching one new group with a core team of experienced members will reduce fatigue for the new group leader. He or she will also be far more willing to serve as the first new leader if the person has a competent launch team (more on this in Chapter 5).

• Every person in your original prototype group may be capable of leading, but will not be ready to lead. Expecting everyone to be excited, competent, and confident to lead a holistic small group is highly assumptive and overly optimistic.

• When a church has more than one holistic small group, coaching is required. It is best to learn how to coach one group before you must coach five or six groups.

Second-Generation Prototype groups

The secondary groups you launch are still quite experimental. They may have been birthed from a healthy prototype group, but they face new challenges. The commitment level of the new group's leadership will be tested. Your own ability to successfully support a small group leader with relational coaching must be developed. Church members who are invited into the groups may radically change the holistic environment. For these reasons, you and your implementation team should still maintain a prototype mindset. Plus, your team still has piles of work to do to properly support the growth of the holistic small group members and leaders.

Step Six: Focus on spiritual freedom and one-on-one discipleship

Before you even *think* about opening your groups to your congregation, your team must develop and implement a relational pathway to spiritual maturity for the new believers. By testing it in the prototype phase, you will shape a culture of discipleship into your holistic small group ministry for future groups to embrace.

Spiritual Freedom

New believers in your prototype groups must experience freedom from satanic strongholds as soon as possible to become effective disciples of Christ. This is typically done in a retreat setting with a mentor, using material such as TOUCH Outreach's *Encounter God Retreat.*

While a weekend retreat won't "fix" the person for life, a focused time out of town and away from everything is life-changing. After a weekend of confession and receiving forgiveness and unconditional love from one's Creator, mentor, and church, a person will naturally take to discipleship like a gosling to water. Without deliverance, the person may never feel the freedom to be bold for Christ, disciple others, become a leader, or pursue spiritual maturity.

If you were to examine world-class small-group-based churches, you would find each one has a deliverance ministry for all incoming group members. It is a normal part of the process of moving deeper

CHAPTER 3 | COMMON MISTAKES THAT PROMOTE LETHARGY AND SMALL GROUP CLOSURE

into the things of God and biblical community. In North America, there is a strong resistance to deliverance, born out of our sophisticated, religious arrogance. In fact, this resistance is a stronghold in and of itself!

Just as God commanded Israel to demolish the strongholds in the Promised Land, your team must create an environment where every small group member can find freedom from satanic strongholds.

One-on-One Discipleship

Second, being a disciple maker profoundly changes a person, transforming him into "a leader of one." The best leadership training you can offer prototype members is to help them become disciple makers. The Christ within is revealed as they pray hard for new believers, love them unconditionally, and teach them the basics of the faith. Discipling a new believer should be something every future leader in your small group ministry should say they have done repeatedly and successfully.

At this stage of implementation, the team should be charged with the task of developing and refining a pathway to spiritual maturity for the new believers in the prototype groups. (For more information on deliverance and relational discipleship, see Chapter 4.)

Step Seven: Implement an effective leader-training process

Wondering when formal small group leader training would come in? Here it is right at the end where it belongs. Prototyping is all about developing healthy small group members. When a couple of them are acting like leaders without the title, it's time to train them to lead a new group. That's right, not everyone in the prototype group should be trained for leadership. Only the ones who are leading out and taking responsibility today as group members should be leading groups tomorrow. Some have taken to holistic small group life and never looked back. These are your first leaders. The people who just went through the motions and never grasped ministry and mission opportunities in the prototype group should—at the very most—become core team members for a new group launch.

In essence, you've been training everyone in the prototype to lead all along. First, you helped your future leaders walk away from a consumer Christianity. Then, you showed them how to live relationally in biblical community outside of church meetings. To develop them further, you helped them embrace a team-based approach to evangelism and one-on-one discipleship, creating leaders of one. And finally, throughout your last year with them, they learned how to facilitate a small group gathering to remain focused on Christ in their midst.

By taking the time to develop a new value system within each prototype member before leadership training, your chances of success in your first groups increase dramatically. Additionally, you can leverage these budding leaders' experience as members and invite them to help the implementation team develop the kind of training new leaders will require for success.

Step Eight: Create a "Boot Camp" for the congregation

If you prototyped for a long enough period of time to get it right, your groups are filled with transformed believers who are on mission for God. These people experience Christ regularly when they meet. They are reaching friends for Christ, helping them find freedom from strongholds, and discipling them to be world changers. The last thing you want to do is dilute this healthy environment by inviting Christian zombies from your congregation to join a group. What you need

CHAPTER 3 | COMMON MISTAKES THAT PROMOTE LETHARGY AND SMALL GROUP CLOSURE

is an interim step for the congregants to protect the health of the first groups and bring the new folks up to speed.

Your implementation team's goal in this first stage of congregational assimilation is clear: implement a two to three month experience for incoming church members to help them see the level of participation required to join a group. If the church members involved are faithful to the Boot Camp gatherings and practical homework assignments given, they will be far less likely to water down the health of your prototype groups.

The process must help incoming believers embrace a new paradigm for kingdom living through discussion (sharing opinions), dialog (discovering a better way together), and practical exercises (tasks they can do to experience what they're hearing about so they can truly learn). The objectives for the Boot Camp are to: help people discover their purpose in life and see how holistic small group life will help them achieve their purpose; give people repeated opportunities to share transparently and receive ministry; help people understand that your church is based on a relationship with Christ, other members, and unchurched friends outside of church meetings; experience the presence, power, and purposes of Christ in a small group environment; and breed a desire for inner healing so they can partner with God and other believers to extend his kingdom.

If you do not require incoming congregational members to move through a Boot Camp experience—which sets the bar higher than having a pulse and a desire to participate—you will increase the potential to pollute your first groups. Your leaders may experience burnout attempting to spoon-feed and motivate consumers. The new group members may feel duped as well, stating they never knew group life would take so much time and require so much of an emotional investment.

Boot Camp content

The best content for a Boot Camp is what you develop. Take the time to explore the lifestyle changes required for church members to become fruitful small group members and work from there. To get the ball rolling, some churches use values-shifting discipleship resources as well as the prayer group strategy found in Chapter 1. Others use the little book I wrote a few years ago called *Community Life 101*. (In Appendix C, you will find the outline from *Life Basic Training*, an assimilation resource written by my father in the early 80s.)

Whatever you use, create an environment where the participants are challenged to start living like healthy small group members before they join a group. Provide time for sharing and activities to experience community life.

Is everyone in the congregation invited to go through the Boot Camp?

Yes, but not all at once. Only a limited number of spaces should be available in the first boot camps. Participation is restrained because you do not want to flood your groups with members when you do not have enough trained leaders. Moreover, you must never add too many church members to an existing group or the evangelistic efforts of that group will suffer or cease. Two or three healthy families moving into each group is about all you should attempt during the first six months after prototyping.

Will everyone who participates graduate and join a group?

Not everyone is ready to face their demons, shed their consumer cloak, and live sacrificially in a biblical community. Therefore, your implementation team must carefully select those who are ready for a new challenge.

As your groups grow and multiply, making room for more people from the congregation, you should increase the number of available seats in your Boot Camp. By using this experience to shape people's values before they move into your groups, you will find your groups do not stagnate.

How many weeks should be scheduled for the Boot Camp experience?

Six to eight weeks is typical. Some churches stretch it to ten weeks. It needs to be long enough for those involved to experience transformation and shed the zombie status.

Where do boot camps meet?

It's best to hold the Boot Camp on your church's campus unless you only have a handful of people participating. This provides ample parking for larger groups, childcare, and a familiar setting. There's no reason you cannot hold them in homes, but you will find that it requires a great deal of support from existing small group hosts.

What does a typical Boot Camp meeting look like?

A short presentation or testimony by a pastor, coach, or small group leader is given based on the subject matter discussed later in smaller groups. This is typically followed by a topical prayer time. Most meetings are 90 minutes in length. Every church's Boot Camp meetings are different, but the goals are similar. Each is designed to expose consumer Christians to the values required to be a kingdom activist and invite them to take the next step in their journey.

Should you call it "Boot Camp?"

The term "Boot Camp" accurately describe the intensity of the process. However, if you call this pre-group assimilation activity *Boot Camp* no one will show up for it! I favor something intriguing and inviting such as *The Foundations Course* or *The Journey.*

When you're implementing small groups organically, your church will look like a horde of obsessed turtles

This strategy is admittedly slow. However, if you stick with it, the plan of action produces healthy pattern groups filled with kingdom activists. Healthy pattern groups prove it can be done in your church, that small groups produce fruit, and small groups are highly missional. The prototype implementation strategy also shows everyone just how easy or difficult the full transition will be.

The congregational assimilation process (Boot Camp) allows for a steady stream of congregational absorption that maintains the health of your groups. As you multiply healthy small groups with new believers from outside your church body, you can invite larger numbers of the congregation to participate in Boot Camp and eventually move into group life. Keep the mix right and the groups will remain healthy. Add too many congregational members, and the groups will lose intimacy and effectiveness in ministry and mission.

Going slow also has another strong benefit. It gives the rest of the church and the lay leaders of existing programs time to see the undeniable power of biblical community and move toward it.

On the following page, you will find a flow chart for an organic holistic small group implementation. Compare it to the one you designed a few pages back to see what you missed or want to add to your implementation process.

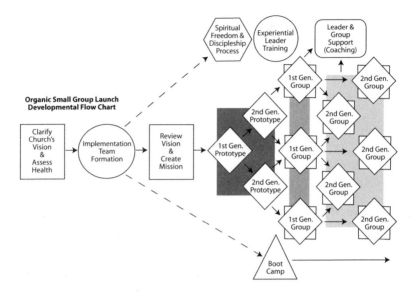

Organic Small Group Launch Developmental Flow Chart

Chart Notes:

1. The implementation team works on the small group ministry, designing and implementing components such as the spiritual freedom weekend, the one-on-one discipleship path, leader training, and the Boot Camp. (The dotted lines and arrows denote these components.)

2. The team also works in the small group ministry (as members of the prototype groups, probable small group leaders, and possible coaches over groups).

3. First- and second-generation prototype groups are open to unchurched people and highly evangelistic in nature. They must grow numerically from conversion growth to develop a healthy DNA as a pattern group.

4. To be invited into a first- or second-generation group, an existing church member must move through the Boot Camp process. Most churches that employ a small group Boot Camp require all members to move through it before entering into holistic small group life and require all transfer growth to go through it.

5. Limiting group multiplication to a Fibonaccii[5] sequence (1-2-3-5-8-13, and so on) allows for healthy expansion. This sequence provides an extra trained group leader to move into the coaching role at each multiplication cycle, creating a classic, highly workable 1:5 oversight (coaching) structure.

110

Do I really need to prototype and move into groups so slowly?

Yes! You really need to rethink your "roll it out in September" strategy and consider the creation of a pattern group. The programmatic, widespread group launch method has a proven track record of creating "sickle cell" small groups that have no missional motivation. Think about it. You need a discipleship pathway, a proven leader training process, a way to coach or support the groups effectively, and money and space in the church calendar. All this takes time.

Keep the cart behind the horse. Place congregational enfolding at the end of the small group development process and remain focused on personal transformation through relational evangelism and one-on-one discipleship. If you prototype, you will establish a level of health in your growing small group ministry that is rarely found in North America.

Let the mega churches toot their horns about how many small groups they have and how great their system is for attracting and retaining consumers. Set your sights higher. Aim for personal transformation and forget the programmatic or campaign-launch strategies geared to pacify consumers. ◆

"I honestly don't think God will grow us beyond our ability to disciple people. And if small groups are our primary context for discipleship, then the number of small groups we have will determine our growth potential as a church." [1]

—Mark Batterson,
Lead Pastor, National Community Church, Washington, D.C.

The naked truth about relational discipleship: the American church doesn't do it

If I were forced to choose the greatest area of neglect in the American small group movement, it would be the issue of discipleship: personally helping believers mature in Christ to become powerful kingdom activists. Thousands of small groups are formed each year in this country, yet the members of these groups will be given no discipleship path, nor will any individual take responsibility for their spiritual maturity. Even voracious self-feeders with a hunger for ministry will struggle in a church that doesn't practice relational discipleship as a core value.

In *Growing True Disciples*, George Barna reveals the pitiful job the church is doing in the area of discipleship:

> Our research shows that churches have a tremendous opportunity to facilitate deeper commitment among believers. Most born-again adults (95 percent) acknowledge that their church encourages spiritual growth. But only half of the believers we interviewed felt that discipleship is one of the two or three highest ministry priorities of their church; the other half said it is just one of many ministries or programs at their church.

Relatively small numbers of born-again adults reported that their church helps them develop specific paths to follow to foster spiritual growth. Slightly less than half told us that their church had identified any spiritual goals, standards, or expectations for the congregation during the past year. (For many people such goals and expectations were mostly limited to exhortations at the end of the sermon. There was no personalization or other, more detailed guidance provided.) Only one out of every five believers stated that their church has some means of facilitating an evaluation of the spiritual maturity or commitment to maturity of congregants. Clearly, the spiritual growth of millions of Christians is being hindered by the lack of detailed assistance and guidance from their churches.[2]

Barna speaks of the American church in general with his research, but the concerns he raises are most important for small group ministry. Without discipleship, it's hard to call your small groups true biblical communities. They are missing a component that shifts them from a weekly meeting of acquaintances to a connected spiritual family.

Discipleship through programs, the group leader, or classes

Meeting or class attendance does not create a fully devoted follower of Christ. These gatherings are missing the one-on-one component that is so powerfully used by God. A person may receive the information in a service and discuss it in his or her small group, yet fail to act upon it. Living out the change or adopting a new lifestyle requires self-induced accountability. The difficult process of examining one's current values—and what drives those values—and discarding them for God's values requires the assistance of a mentor or someone who is further along in his or her spiritual journey.

Many pastors agree, but they still miss the point of a transformational relationship as a life-giving part of community life. It's apparent they're attempting to get the job done with the least amount of hassle by launching programs to move members through a discipleship process. Within a calendar year, they discover the effectiveness is debatable and participation is limited. Like so many others before them, they learn that if discipleship is not delivered through a one-on-one relationship, it will always be a program that never gains traction.

Consider your own walk with Christ. When did you experience the greatest season of personal growth? Was it when you were sitting in a classroom or a meeting? Probably not. Someone adopted you and poured his or her life into you. The person showed you by example and through mentoring who God is and what Christ could do through you. Because of this, you grew like a weed, right? Transformational discipleship occurs within the context of communion with God and community with a more mature believer.

In my little book on coaching small groups, I wrote about one of my mentors. Greg is an ordinary guy with an extraordinary desire to help others grow in Christ. Despite my pugnacious disposition, he saw potential and attached himself to me in 1992 for three years.

I didn't realize I was being discipled. I just knew an older guy wanted to spend time with me and valued my friendship. He asked my opinion about things that were of interest to me (sports cars and computers) as well as deep spiritual things I never thought about before. After a few meetings over coffee, he asked me if we could spend a Saturday morning together cleaning out his garage. Although I thought that request was odd, I agreed to help him because I wanted to spend time with him.

As we installed shelving, Greg asked me for permission to share a personal observation about my prevailing life attitude. He said that he saw a great deal of potential within me for personal growth and success. I could not see it because I filtered everything through a cloud of bitterness. When he asked me if I could see that within my own life, I distinctly remember telling him, "Opinions are like one's derrière. Everyone has one but they stink and should be kept to one's self." (Of course, my language was not nearly that polite.)

Greg had thick skin and wasn't put off by my retort. With a belly laugh, he said, "See what I mean?"

What drew me to Greg was his ability to be outspoken and brash. Looking back, I clearly see he was exactly what I needed. It's as if God brought an older, fiery man into my world to show me I wasn't all that hot. That terse response was a test, and he passed it and many others. In the days and weeks to follow, he earned the right to speak into very deep parts of my life, help me forgive others, and work out God's calling on my life.

To this very day, Greg's fingerprints can be found on my life and ministry. He taught me how to ask deep, penetrating questions to help others discover the root of their issues. He explained passages in the Bible with excitement. He showed me how to think strategically about a small group to see the possibilities for future leadership development. He also showed me how to earn my wife's respect and deepen it through a lifetime of servanthood. Most importantly, Greg modeled a lifestyle of prayer. We prayed together regularly and I learned how to commune with God.

People will never receive this kind of personal development in programs or formal gatherings. They won't receive it by attending a small group either. For discipleship to take hold among your small group members, one-on-one mentoring isn't an option. It's a requirement.

"We have a double-duty program to explain the basics of the faith"

A few months ago, I served as a table assistant in our church's Alpha program.[3] At the time, my church used this resource as an outreach program and a pathway for new members to discover foundational biblical truths.

My table consisted of a young married couple who grew up in our church as childhood sweethearts, three young-adult Christians who have been members for three or four years, and an unchurched guy who was taken to church as a child but never gained a guiding faith in Christ. Our table leader was an amazing young woman who did an excellent job of making everyone at the table feel comfortable enough to share his or her true feelings about the subject of the video presentation. As her assistant, my role was to ask others at the table what they thought of the topic and restrain myself from balking at anything odd that came out of the mouths of those at our table.

Eight weeks into the program, we watched Nicky Gumbel provide an excellent presentation surrounding the authenticity and validity of the Bible. Then, over dessert and coffee we discussed our opinions about the Bible's role in our lives. When asked what they thought about the Bible's inerrancy, one of the church members (a guy who grew up in a denominational church) said, "I can't imagine every single thing in the Bible is accurate considering all those authors and the time frame in which it was written. Frankly, that doesn't matter though. It's all good stuff that I need to apply to my life." Then another church member (who grew up in my church) commented, "I agree with you. Take Noah and the ark, for example. From his perspective on the ark, the earth probably looked flooded. But that was just his perception. There's no way every single species of land animal made it to the ark. I don't think the entire earth flooded."

Although I remained quiet and smiled warmly, on the inside I was about to come unglued! How on earth could faithful members of our church spit out this opinionated swill as if it were gospel truth? I've heard our pastor cover this in great depth from the pulpit, and we talk about it in our small groups all the time! How could they possibly think that the Bible isn't accurate? What will they challenge next? Jesus being raised from the dead? The ascension? The promise of his glorious return?

In just a few weeks' time, I discovered that each church member at my Alpha table showed great leadership potential. Each should be leading a small group or something far greater. Yet they are blown here and there by their own doctrine.[4] What these believers desperately need is a spiritual mentor to walk them past their assumptions to understand the truth about God and the validity of the Word (among many other things). Had our church implemented and refined a relational discipleship path within our small group ministry, these believers would be in a very different place in their spiritual walk.

In *Authentic Spiritual Mentoring*, Larry Kreider speaks directly to the shift in thinking the American church must make about discipleship:

> There is a desperate need for spiritually mature men and women to mentor younger Christians, helping them to clarify what really matters in life and work. Spiritual mentors

who act as mature coaches can help younger believers achieve their dreams and visions and feel connected as they integrate life and work and grow to maturity.

Instead of deep and nurturing relationships, too often in today's Church a believer is encouraged to participate in church services, Bible studies, para-church organizations or evangelistic ministries in order to bolster his or her faith and "grow strong in the Lord." The theory is that more teaching from God's Word plus more ministry participation equals more spiritual maturity. As important as these involvements may be, such a faulty supposition leads to believers inhaling message after message, book after book, CD after CD, seminar after seminar, all in order to fill a void for real relationship.

The result is a Christian who becomes fat spiritually and fails to interpret what he or she is learning so that he or she can pass it on to others. This person doesn't know how to meaningfully or sacrificially impart his or her life to others because he or she has never been properly parented. Without a role model, he or she remains a spiritual infant, needing to be spoon-fed by the pastor or other Christian worker.[5]

As we wrapped up our eleven sessions of Alpha, I asked everyone at my table if they would like to visit a small group. I told them I coached four dynamically different groups where they would find a spiritual family in which to belong. The unchurched guy swapped cell phone numbers with me and visited my small group the next week. He's hungry to learn more about God and wants a deeper relationship with his Creator.

The church members at my table showed no urgency to visit a group. I learned each of them had been in a small group for a couple of years but dropped out. Because they never developed deep relationships as a member, being in a group was no longer a priority. Think about it. If a small group is just another meeting where the more mature members do not have a sacrificial interest in your personal growth, you wouldn't prioritize it either.

"Our small group leaders are the disciple makers"

At this point, you may be thinking, "Our group leaders are discipling the members of their groups, just like Jesus did with his disciples." If your small group leaders have full-time jobs, a household to run, and a family; if they volunteer on weekends for your services in some capacity and maintain a hobby or enjoy a sport for exercise, they cannot and *will not* disciple all the members of their group. In fact, they may not have the time and energy to train an apprentice.

The members of the group must take responsibility for one another. By doing so, the members keep growing because they must stay ahead of the persons being mentored. When members mentor, leader burnout is reduced. And finally, when members disciple one another, the group moves from being a meeting-centered gathering to a kingdom-centered community.

On the other side of the coin, the new believers learn through demonstration that the Christian life is characterized by thinking beyond their own needs or desires. They watch the more mature Christians reach friends for Christ and disciple them.

"We offer elective classes"

Some churches offer classes for various areas of interest or need and call this discipleship. However, these classes do not produce widespread transformation among small group members. As you have probably discovered, only an interested few show up to an opt-in class. Everyone else stays home to watch CSI reruns. Class-based training also runs a risk of being far too cognitive. People make a permanent shift in values through repeated experiences, not a lecture mandating change in one area of life.

Stand-alone classroom teaching also reinforces consumerism by its design and the way it is typically marketed: "If you want to learn how to study your Bible, improve your marriage, or sort out your finances, show up on Wednesday nights this fall." The call is to take what one wants, which may be vastly different from what one truly needs.

Our church has a marriage class that was life-changing when my wife and I went through it as participants. We were so pleased with the results that we helped facilitate it the following year and invited numerous couples we knew from the congregation that would benefit from it. However, the couples in the greatest danger of separation or divorce never attended the course. Even though they have heard that each couple has their own little table set apart from everyone else and they didn't have to share with the whole group, they were still unwilling to participate. What was missing? Genuine relationships with older married couples in their small group. While mentors cannot provide professional counseling or the depth of information that a marriage course or a counselor offers, their role as a mentor is a key to helping the couple see the value of a marriage course or formal counseling.

A few pages back, I mentioned that Greg helped me earn my wife's respect. One afternoon, he asked me about my desires for my marriage. When I said I wanted a submissive wife, Greg said, "Earning your wife's respect to the point of submission doesn't come easily. I'm not sure you're ready to work that hard for it."

Piquing my interest, I invited him to tell me more. Greg took out his Bible and showed me that as the head of my household, I was to lay down my life for my wife the way Jesus did for his bride, the church. This scriptural application was powerful, and I wanted to be that kind of husband.

After a brief discussion about the chores I was to do around the house, he made a suggestion. Greg instructed me to empty the kitchen trash can each time I saw it fill up (not when Etna asked me to do it). He also instructed me not to bring attention to the fact that I had done it if she wasn't watching. The first part was not that hard, but the second part required self-restraint. Greg helped me see that Etna serves me all the time without bringing attention to what she does and I should do the same.

Two weeks later, I proudly shared that I had completed both parts of the task and was ready to move to the next level. Knowing I loved my sports car and washed it by hand every Saturday morning above every other priority, Greg challenged me to focus on Etna's car. I was to give it a complete detail job replete with a wash, buff, wax, and shampooed floor mats.

As I cleaned Etna's car that next weekend, I was convicted by my own neglect. Her car had not been properly detailed since it was driven off the dealership lot. After ten grueling hours of work, I dragged myself into the house at dusk and flopped onto the couch in a heap. I thought, "Earning respect is simply exhausting."

The next morning we went out to my car and she asked, "Why is your car still dirty?" When I told her that her car needed a thorough cleaning and there wasn't time to work on my car, she gave me a kiss

THE NAKED TRUTH ABOUT RELATIONAL DISCIPLESHIP

and said, "Thank you for loving me more than your car."

The next time Greg and I met, he told me Etna caught him after a church service and said I was turning into "a new and improved husband." Then he told me something I've never forgotten: "Now you must keep it up. Serve her sacrificially for the rest of your life. Give her the best piece of steak when you're grilling. Empty the dishwasher when you find clean dishes in it. Do a load of laundry before she has a chance to get to it. Sweep or vacuum the floors without being asked. Wash the dog every two weeks like clockwork. Bring her flowers between her birthday and Valentine's Day just to show her you love her. Make your own honey-do list for yourself. You know, consider her needs before your own in every area of life. She will then gladly submit to your authority because it's easy to follow someone who serves you and consistently proves his love with action."

Did Etna and I need that marriage class twelve years later? You bet! Years ago, Greg helped me see how important it is to keep my marriage a priority. But the marriage class did not walk me through the values shift required to discard my selfishness and become a servant to my wife. Nor did it give me a desire to befriend young husbands and repeat what Greg did with me. That was accomplished through a long-term relationship with someone who cared enough to mentor me and help me adopt those values.

Mentoring drives and heightens everything you do for your members, such as parenting or marriage-enrichment courses. Without a spiritual parent who will speak into a person's life, the right people never show up to opt-in classes or programs, nor do they retain what they learn. They need the encouragement and accountability that comes through a mentoring relationship.

Should we disciple members to gain more small group leaders?

An obvious sign of weakness in any small group ministry is the absence of eager group members who desire to lead. Had the church leaders prioritized mentoring and discipleship when they launched groups, this weakness would not exist. The root of the issue is really quite simple: If believers have never been shown how to live a life of victory over sin and become fruitful in ministry and mission, they'll never possess the confidence or competence to become small group leaders.

This realization has motivated many church leaders to implement a discipleship pathway after the fact to correct their leadership problem. Sadly, they don't produce disciples or leaders for two interconnected reasons. First, their motivation must be called into question if it is based on building their own castle instead of God's kingdom. Second, the members of the groups were never challenged to take on this level of personal commitment and sacrifice when small groups were introduced.

"God, please bless my structure"

When I was a teenager, I asked God repeatedly if he would make me wealthy so I could serve him unencumbered by financial adversity. It was a prayer I voiced regularly through my adolescence and into my first years of marriage. However, servanthood was not my primary motive. As a child, I dreamed of being rich enough to fill a seven-car garage with exotic sports cars—one for every day of the week. My prayer as a teen was an extension of this root desire. As you can easily surmise, God did not give me this kind of wealth because it was a selfish request.

Implementing a discipleship pathway to correct a structural issue is just as selfish. If your primary motivation is anything other than equipping the saints whom God has entrusted to you for the work of their ministry,[6] you're spinning your wheels. Don't expect God to bless your discipleship efforts and don't expect the members of the groups to line up for new rules you've added late into the game. Most folks are smart enough to see how their participation will primarily make the organization larger, not help them grow. No one wants to be a cog in your church's ever-expanding clockworks.

To enjoy a powerful anointing in discipleship, your motivation must be to be obedient to the commands of Christ.[7] Love your small group members enough to help them become mature in their faith, and make these things your motivation.

Wait. There's more!

I've given this issue a great deal of thought. While writing the outline for this chapter, it occurred to me that discipling members with the proper motivation (extending the kingdom) and with the proper delivery system (mentoring) is just like buying a set of Ginsu knives. Remember the infomercial from so many years ago? If you buy the amazing set of ever-sharp kitchen knives—a fantastic value at any price—you'll receive a bottle opener *and* two other cool kitchen contraptions for free!

And so it goes with making genuine disciples through mentoring for the sake of the kingdom, not to fortify one's castle. The model churches I mentioned in the introduction have *waiting lists* of members who hunger to lead their own groups! While each church organizes their groups differently with unique discipleship priorities, they all have one thing in common: each is motivated to develop people into mature disciple-makers, not just train future leaders.

Small group leadership is a free "bonus gift" for the church that brings believers into maturity where they see their spiritual potential and live it out.

Missing Components

I've asked a number of pastors about their church's motivation for discipleship and found it to be kingdom-driven. Their hunger to help people discover their role in the kingdom and become a fully devoted follower of Christ is genuine—yet their groups are stuck. By digging a little deeper into their process, I discovered that their discipleship path is weak in two areas: deliverance from satanic strongholds and relational evangelism. Memorizing Scripture, understanding the basics of the faith, and learning denominational distinctives are important, but these things alone do not help a new Christian become victorious in life and enjoy a lifetime of ministry and mission.

My father uses 1 John 2:12-14 in his values-shifting discipleship material[8] to describe the three basic levels of spiritual maturity. I often assess a church's discipleship pathway with this passage:

I write to you, dear children, because your sins have been forgiven on account of his name.
I write to you, fathers, because you have known him who is from the beginning.
I write to you, young men, because you have overcome the evil one.
I write to you, dear children, because you have known the Father.

I write to you, fathers, because you have known him who is from the beginning.

I write to you, young men, because you are strong, and the word of God lives in you, and you have overcome the evil one.

This passage shows how people mature in Christ and the milestones they will need to cross successfully:

The Child: One who knows God as "Abba." This believer knows she is unconditionally loved by God and fully accepted by him even though she still battles with destructive and sinful habits or wounds from the past.

The Young Man: One who is triumphant over Satan's schemes and is free of besetting sin. Discovering where he has been deceived and owning up to sinful patterns cuts straight through religious pride and arrogance. Freedom from strongholds gives a believer a hunger to know more of God and do his will.

The Father: One who reaches others for Christ and successfully mentors them. When someone takes responsibility for a younger brother in Christ, his prayer life increases and his faith will be tested. This kind of tempering provides a mature believer with a lifelong ministry and mission.

Can Christians have satanic strongholds?

When Israel was given "the land of goats and bees" (milk and honey), they were told to drive out the giants that inhabited their land. They ignored them for a while and suffered the consequences. These strongholds were a nagging problem until they eradicated the enemy, their livestock, and their homes and farms. Canaan was indeed given to Israel as the Promised Land, but it required a great deal of cleanup. In other words, God listed the land on the spiritual real estate market as "a phenomenal property with great potential if the new owners will invest sweat equity."

My story

I made a profession of faith at six years of age and was water baptized when I was ten. When I was twenty-four, I recommitted my life to Christ and put away many childish things. However, there were pockets of unforgiveness and resentment in my life that I did not fully recognize. The hurts were simply too deep to fully comprehend and release to the Lord, so I pushed them down deep within myself and tried to ignore them.

For many years, Satan wrote checks on those buried accounts. Through sheer will power, I did not fall back into the old sinful habits of my youth, but I was attacked with horrible temptation from time to time. Even though I successfully resisted, the battle in my mind kept me from enjoying my life in Christ, For many years, I felt defeated and unworthy to be used by God. Before I found freedom from my strongholds, my walk with Christ could be characterized as controlled torment. Resisting temptation without addressing the root issue was simply exhausting.

So let me answer my own question. Yes. Christians can have pockets of satanic activity in their life. I've yet to meet any person in this broken world who does not have some sort of deep issue with a parent, sibling, or relative to work through. Bitterness, anger, and resentment manifest themselves in addiction, depression, a defeatist's attitude, arrogance, or avarice.

Some sort of deliverance weekend and inner healing ministry for small group members must be engineered into your discipleship pathway. If you do not provide this very early in the process, you will discover a lack of enthusiasm in the balance of the discipleship path and especially the evangelism component.

Facing one's demons makes one bold for Christ

Before the economic collapse of 2008, I asked a long-time friend how he was doing. In passing, he told me he received a new position and an increase in pay at his company. Some of my friends would have shared this as a praise report, but not this friend. No amount of advancement or pay seems to make him happy. If he received a fat bonus to take the position and was given double the salary, he would have commented, "I deserved more" or "It's about time they recognized what a great employee I am compared to everyone else in my department."

Last week, I spoke to him again and asked about his work. Although he's made it through two rounds of layoffs, he complained that he is overworked, undervalued, and, of course, underpaid. Once again, others would have a heart of gratitude that they were still valued enough by their company to be employed in such tough financial times. Because of his stronghold, he perceives every good thing as negative. He harbors a great deal of resentment toward his parents for the preferential treatment given to his siblings. These deep wounds of resentment are the root of his critical spirit and negative outlook on life.

I love my friend and make it a point to visit with him as often as I can. However, his wounds have made him a very lonely person. He doesn't maintain friendships with other men his age. He keeps everyone at arm's length and rarely shares deeply with others. His strongholds have also neutralized his ability to develop relationships with unchurched people. Without victory over this issue, he may never realize his full potential in Christ.

A person who walks through life with suppressed wounds has nothing exciting to talk about. Everything is filtered through unresolved hurts, making the person's life very unattractive to other believers. This person may have a good story to tell about the day she gave her life to Christ and how much she values her paid-up spiritual fire-insurance policy, but her story is not that attractive unless the hearer has a terminal illness and wants to know what to expect when he or she reaches "the other side." Until small group members have experienced freedom from strongholds, don't expect them to ooze God's joy out of every pore. Boldness comes when a believer has faced his or her demons to find healing from hurts and wounds.

Deliverance outside of biblical community

I'm often asked why I only discuss deliverance for committed small group members and not the entire church congregation. I find my basis in Scripture:

> Be sober, be watchful. Your adversary the devil prowls around like a roaring lion, seeking some *one* to devour.
> (1 Peter 5:8, *Revised Standard Version*, emphasis mine)

On my last trip to Kruger Park, a South African game preserve, I observed the way the animals protect themselves from lions. When we saw a baboon, we'd also see more in the area because they live in troops. While the playful primates jumped on our car and romped in the grass beside the road, another, perched high in a tree above us, served as a lookout for lions. The wart hogs we saw were plentiful in number as well. When frightened, these hairy little swine point their tails straight up in the air before running into the heavy brush. Any wart hog nearby seeing that tail go up in the air knows there's danger close by and its time to play follow the leader. The impala, springbok, zebra, and kudu all do the same thing. They travel in small groupings because if they travel alone they will surely become a tasty meal.

Luke illustrates how important it is for Christians to remain in community for their own protection with his account of Jesus delivering a demon-possessed man:

> For Jesus had commanded the evil spirit to come out of the man. Many times it had seized him, and though he was chained hand and foot and kept under guard, he had broken his chains and had been driven by the demon *into solitary places.*   (Luke 8:29, emphasis mine)

Satan's scheme has always been to divide and conquer. If he can drive a person into a solitary place, he's free to work him over and deceive him into exchanging the truth for a lie. In both of these Scriptures and many others, we see the defensive nature of living in biblical community. There's protection in numbers.

A church that encourages members to sign up for deliverance ministry without small group involvement and a mentor to help them walk out their freedom in Christ invites Satan to attack them because they will be alone and vulnerable after the event.

The great omission

The other missing component in many churches' discipleship path is relational evangelism. Once again, churches may offer evangelism classes or a program, but this is not what I'm writing about. These are optional for the membership at large and rarely help small group members understand the impact their biblical community can have on their efforts to reach friends for Christ. The goal of a discipleship component for relational evangelism must be to create an environment for a new believer that teaches him or her how to reach a friend for Christ and disciple the person as a mentor. If this is integrated into your discipleship process, it will become a cultural lifestyle for your small group members.

My definition of relational evangelism may be quite different from yours, so let's get on the same page. When people are reached for Christ with relational evangelism as it pertains to small-group-based ministry, the following principles are employed:

Build a true friendship

Every day, we are bombarded with scams through email offers, our mailbox, and the telephone. I hate shakedowns by total strangers. The last thing an unbeliever wants is someone trying to sell his or her brand of religion with friendly manipulation. Relational evangelism's foundation is built upon a genuine friendship.

As I consider my friendships with my unchurched buddies, I find that we have one or more interests in common. Initially, we spend most of our time talking about that hobby or activity, and it is the basis for our friendship. I own a mid-engine sports car, maintain a marine aquarium, and I'm now crafting wood pens at a friend's woodworking shop. Some of my unchurched friends also have one or two of these things in common, and God has used these hobbies to bring us together.

I am not their friend solely because they need Christ or biblical community and I'm God's man for the project. What began as a common interest in a hobby is now something precious—a real friendship. If one of my friends—who just happens to be unchurched or doesn't believe in Christ as Lord—decided to end our relationship, I would be devastated. While I haven't asked any of my friends if they would be deeply hurt if I turned my back on them, I firmly believe they would say the same thing.

I am also not the kind of person that only befriends people who are easy to be around. A few of my friends are rough around the edges. Others are downright abrasive. Christians I know would never spend time with them because of their bad habits, foul mouth, and opinionated responses to just about everything. For some reason, I enjoy being around people who could care less what others think.

I also befriend others that God specifically tells me to befriend. Often, we have nothing in common, but they are desperate for a friend and I make friends easily. So we spend time together doing things that everyone does—watching a movie, eating dinner, going to car shows, taking in a ball game, or whatever the person or I need or want to do.

Everyone needs friends and wants genuine relationships. Making friends and deepening those friendships without a personal agenda or expectation is what makes relational evangelism fun. I am not in charge of the spiritual aspects of the relationship. God is doing something in the person, but I usually don't see it until it's too late to control it, direct it, or take credit. I do see God using me in subtle ways though, and this has helped me clearly see the partnership with the Lord that I provide.

Show your weakness

Recently, I heard one of my friends comment, "The thing I hate about religious people is their arrogance. They think because they are 'born again,' they are superior in some way to me. Isn't pride a sin?"

He's right. Many Christians are so proud of the free gift of salvation given to them that they wear it like an Armani suit. For a healthy friendship to exist, there must be reciprocity. I help you out with something and you invite me over for dinner to show your appreciation. I ask you to take me to the airport at 4 a.m. to catch an overseas flight, and I in turn ask you if I can help you clean out your garage the next weekend. Your wife is stranded at the mall with a dead battery when you're still at work, and I head that direction to get her car started and follow her home. Or I share the fact that I'm barely making ends meet with debt and you offer to help me figure out a budget and stick to it ... and you're my unchurched friend. This is a healthy friendship that's headed somewhere.

Everyone has needs. Showing one's weakness is an important part of building a true friendship. It's also the number one reason the unchurched friends of Christians don't come to Christ. They don't experience the Christian as a humble person who just happens to be saved by grace. They see an arrogant religious individual who is oblivious of their pride. For friendship evangelism to work, the believer must ask others for help and reveal his or her vulnerable side.

Cross-pollinate

At some point in the friendship, introducing your new friend to your existing friends is not only appropriate; it's vital to the relationship. Without opportunities to spend time with me and my Christian friends, my unchurched friend is not seeing "the real me."

This is where small group involvement must be more than a weekly meeting. Dave Earley, a pastor and author of many small group leadership books, wrote, "First, win the person as a friend. Then win them as a friend to your small group. Then they will be won to Christ."[9] For relational evangelism to naturally move to that important next level, the unbeliever must be brought into a biblical community through friendships with other small group members.

Relational evangelism is net fishing, not angling with a line and a hook. It involves time and multiple people in the process. When the person trusts Christ, the members of the group will become the convert's new spiritual family. All will feel they had a part in bringing the person to Christ and all will feel varying levels of responsibility to help the person grow spiritually.

When a person is won to Christ outside of a biblical community, the chances of survival are slim. The first time the person who is discipling the convert shows his or her humanity, the new believer may fall away. Or, the disciple maker becomes controlling because he or she is the only influence in the new Christian's life. It's always more profitable to work the net and reach people for Christ and disciple them in the context of a spiritual family.

Refuse to be a spiritual chameleon

If you and I became friends, we'd probably share areas of spiritual weakness, what we think God is saying to us, and what we're hoping God will do in us and through us in our work, families, and relationships. This is what healthy Christian friends do with one another. We talk about our faith and our struggles with our faith.

However, when Christians spend time with unchurched friends, many do not share matters of spiritual importance. They are confident

CHAPTER 4 | THE AMERICAN CHURCH DOESN'T DO IT

the unbeliever will not understand, and they'd be right! But there's incredible power to be a witness for Christ when a believer speaks to his or her unbelieving friends in the manner used when interacting with Christian friends.

I've had numerous unchurched friends turn to me and say, "You know, I can tell you really love God and I can see he really loves you. I don't have that with God." If I had not shared what I wanted God to do in my life to be more Christ-like and what I was leaning on him to do as my Master, they would think I'm no different than anyone else. Sharing with my unchurched friends in the same way I share with my fellow small group members builds a contrast for the unbeliever that is genuine and attractive.

Christian duplicity sorts itself out nicely when a believer creates genuine friendships with unchurched persons and then cross-pollinates those relationships with other believers. I firmly believe that this is a key to relational evangelism. After all, acting one way with Christian friends and another with unbelieving friends is the second greatest reason that Christians do not see long-time friends and family members come to Christ. (The first reason would be that they've never met a Christian before.)

The shift away from duplicity is not an easy one to make, but it must be made. When a believer speaks of the same things to his unbelieving friends as he does with other believers, that Christian's ability to share God's love with others effectively increases tenfold.

Call their bluff if they say they believe in God

Many of my unchurched friends say they believe in God. It's likely an impersonal view, but it's a base belief or an ideal they hold. So I find God-sized problems and ask them to pray with me for answers, solutions, or flat-out miracles. Do they look at me funny when I casually ask them to say a prayer every day for something in my life? Oh yeah. I'm challenging them to pray to God based on their previous comments. Most have never been asked to do this before, but now is the time as far as I'm concerned. I call their bluff to see just how much faith they possess.

If nothing comes up in my life that needs prayer, I know they will eventually hit a brick wall with their job, spouse, finances, or a child. It's just a matter of time. When calamity strikes, I ask the person if he or she has asked God for help. After all, the person believes in God, right? My friends usually say they aren't used to doing this or feel "weird" when they try to pray. My reply? "God is always listening for you to speak to him and he's always interested in blessing you ... and he talks back! I hear him all the time."

When my non-Christian friends start praying, they start believing in something they can't see or touch, which is faith. When they grow in faith that God hears and loves them, they're walking toward the cross whether they know it or not. Combined with the other principles, this naturally moves people from unawareness to awareness to receptivity to a hunger to establish a connection through Christ.

I just love what happens when my unbelieving friends start praying and hanging out with other members of my small group. The combination turns them into small group members. They eagerly share the icebreaker for the group and bring snacks without being asked. They serve others between meetings. They open their homes for group meetings. Soon enough, they make a public profession of faith in Christ and hunger to know more about God and this Christ that has done so much for them.

Pray for yourself as much as you pray for lost friends

When I pray, I always have something to say to God about the spiritual condition of my unbelieving friend, but too little to say about myself. Through trial and error, I have discovered that I must pray hard for myself instead of focusing on the besetting sins of others. I've made it a habit to pray about the following when I think about my unsaved friends.

My depravity. My accountability partner constantly tells me, "You are one sick puppy." He's absolutely right. I am a broken mess of a person in desperate need of a Savior. When I consistently pray about the messed up way I think and act, God graciously gives me humility.

The way I view others. In the natural, I view the brokenness of others through my own brokenness. However, when I petition God for his view of a person—broken yet deeply and unconditionally loved—it drastically changes my view. Judgment is transformed into compassion.

My reactions. I'm constantly praying I will have an insightful response to pointed questions about God, the Bible, my own walk with Christ, and left-field questions about immorality among pastors and priests. Knowing the right thing to say is about knowledge. How and when to say the right thing is something else altogether.

Relational evangelism is caught, not taught

These principles are not new or innovative, yet they're wholly ignored in most discipleship tracks. We've exhausted one reason: small groups were created for consumers, not producers. If moving through a discipleship process and taking on what feels like a heavy burden of evangelism is required for membership, few will sign up. No one has shown them just how fun relational evangelism can be when God is doing the hard work of conviction and we're enjoying time with friends.

American Christians are cocooned within a religious subculture. Many have no friendships outside the four walls of the church building or their small group. What they desperately need is someone to show them how it's done to give them a new paradigm for evangelism. That's one reason mentoring is so important.

Do something different to get different results

In many churches, pastors provide quality teaching from the pulpit that would be transformational if those hearing it would make personal application. A majority of these churches provide a small group environment for believers to process and implement what they are learning. The American church has done everything it knows how to do with a top-down approach to discipleship, yet it is not turning congregants into highly motivated and successful ministers of the gospel.

For significant change to take place in your church in the area of discipleship, you must acknowledge that your current ministry model is deficient. The Sunday sermon and small group "one-two punch" does not possess enough power to disciple people. The teaching-application model should not be abandoned by any means, but it's time to add the missing components that create a disciple-making environment.

Do your small group members want to be discipled by a mentor?
Barna's comments on his research indicate that the members of

your church want discipleship and many are open to being mentored as well:

> Nine out of ten said that if their church helped them iden-
> tify specific spiritual-growth goals to pursue, they would at
> least listen to the advice and follow parts, if not all of it. Very
> few people (5 percent) said they would flat-out ignore the
> advice. Only one out of every one hundred believers said they
> would leave the church if it tried to deliver such an analysis.
> (Let me emphasize that this relates to congregant-specific ad-
> vice for spiritual growth, not general, congregation-wide
> exhortation, or pronouncements.)
>
> A majority (55 percent) of the adults who indicated their
> interest in advice on how to improve their spiritual life also
> said that if the church matched them up with a spiritual
> mentor or coach, they would be more likely to pursue the
> changes suggested to them. Only 7 percent indicated that a
> mentor or coach would make them less likely to pursue the
> growth suggestions.[10]

Last year, I met a man in his fifties named Brett. I am not sure he took an instant liking to me, but I decided I wanted him as a friend five minutes into our first conversation. We shared jokes, poked fun at our other friend Mark as if we were tag-team wrestlers, and talked for an hour about our favorite exotic cars. A few weeks later, he called me and said, "Hey, this is 'Uncle Brett.' Can you drive over to Mark's place next Saturday so we can work on your brakes?"

Days later, I was up to my elbows in grease as Brett showed me how to swap out the brake pads, rotors, and bleed the brake lines on my project car. He did the first wheel while I watched him and asked questions. When he finished, he said, "Now you do the other three. Don't worry. I'll watch you to make sure you don't !#$% up and kill yourself on the way home." (For some reason, guys that have the skills to fix cars also have the uncanny ability to work four-letter words into every sentence when teaching a mechanical newbie.)

What did I ask for the next Christmas? A set of metric tools! Brett showed me that any village idiot could do a brake job on a car if he has the time, the desire, and a little help from an experienced friend.

I firmly believe every person wants someone to adopt him or her as a nephew or niece. It feels great to know that you are valuable enough to receive the attention of an older, wiser person. Mentoring is definitely something your small group members will be interested in if they are approached at the right time.

Do your small group members want to mentor others?

If I were to ask the members of my small group to mentor someone, I know what would happen. Everyone would shout, "Run away!" with a lousy British accent. Teaching someone how to do a brake job is easy for a guy whose been working on cars for many years and was taught through mentoring. Christians today have never been mentored, so they cannot envision themselves in the role. The request alone would scare the wee out of them!

For this reason, you cannot mandate mentoring as a new requirement for small group membership. Potential mentors must move into their new role naturally, and there are ways to create this environment, which I'll share in the rest of the chapter.

What to do about it

Implementing a mentor-protégé discipleship process in your small groups when the value for it does not currently exist is not impossible, but it ain't easy. Members do not view themselves as a mentor nor do they see opportunities to mentor within their group, even though both perspectives could not be further from the truth. Therefore, implementation must be far more strategic. I recommend evangelizing your way out of your discipleship conundrum.

When a sixteen-year-old girl gives birth and is determined to raise that bundle of joy instead of giving the child up for adoption, she will need a great deal of support from her parents. By the time her child becomes a toddler, the juvenile mother will have matured in many ways. Taking responsibility for another life changes a person, doesn't it?

This is where you should begin with your church's relational discipleship implementation strategy. Show the members of your small groups how to befriend unchurched people and lead them to the cross. When they have reached a friend for Christ, they'll have a natural sense of urgency to help their friend grow, and both will mature rapidly.

Will small group members be fearful about discipling someone when they've never been discipled? Absolutely. First-time parents are scared too, but they still have babies and boldly embrace the journey of raising a child. If you've done a good job of articulating your discipleship path and provide corporate support for the process, first-time mentors will find it less stressful.

Determine your goals for discipleship

More than 80 percent of the members of Xenos Christian Fellowship in Columbus, Ohio, are involved in discipleship as a mentor or protégé. As far as I am concerned, this church is doing a better job of producing disciples than any other American church I have found.

Dennis McCallum and Jessica Lowery have written about their church's discipleship process in *Organic Disciplemaking*. Their goals include permanent change in the following areas:

Character: possessing a good personal walk with God, becoming a loving person with successful relationships, exchanging selfishness for others-centeredness, freedom from discrediting sin, manifesting the fruit of the Spirit, and a relatively stable emotional life.

Understanding: a thoroughly developed Christian worldview, good theology, knowledge of the Bible, and the ability to use the Bible in ministry, wisdom, discernment, and resistance to false teaching.

Ministry capability: evangelism, pastoring others, personal discipleship, teaching or discussion leading, etc. (Spiritual growth is never complete when it only benefits ourselves. We are created to give love through serving others.)[11]

Xenos has worked to refine these goals and state them in a way that is measurable. Every mentor knows that his or her role is to help a disciple live out the three goals above. This is done through the following relational steps:

- Friendship-building
- A regular meeting time
- Enhanced, interpersonal sharing
- Appropriate biblical and theological content to study together

- Times of prayer
- Counseling and helping the disciple in areas of weakness
- Helping the disciple develop a ministry
- Releasing the disciple to pursue a life of service to God[12]

The first thing you must do is to create measurable goals for your discipleship path. This will help you determine the required components and determine if your process works. Then you must determine the level of support required by the church staff and other ministries. The mentor can help his or her disciple develop a deep prayer life without help from anyone. Helping that same disciple find freedom from strongholds will probably entail a retreat sponsored by the church where the mentor can walk the disciple through a time of confession followed by ministry. Achieving your discipleship goals will have an impact on your church calendar and budget and involve more people and resources than just those in your small group ministry. Count the costs carefully before you proceed, but don't let a high cost or changes in your church's calendar or budget dissuade you from making disciples.

Climbing a mountain of spiritual maturity

Imagine you were climbing Mount Everest. Being a smart climber, you know you need a guide who has made the journey to help you reach the summit. You meet your guide at the base camp and together you review the map to discover your current position, the equipment you have brought with you, and the path you will take up the mountain to the next camp. Others are climbing with you, and they have joined you in an instructional time with a veteran Everest climber. He or she explains all sorts of things about the entire climb and what to expect at each camp.

An effective discipleship path that is corporately supported and mentor-driven will have a series of camps and hikes. The camps are mid-sized groupings of mentors and disciples where the process is reviewed and the next steps are shared. Then the disciples meet with their mentors and hike to the next campsite, where they learn about the next part of the journey. While the discipleship path's summit will vary from church to church, it must include the disciple maturing to the point of becoming a mentor and discipling others to passionately pursue ministry.

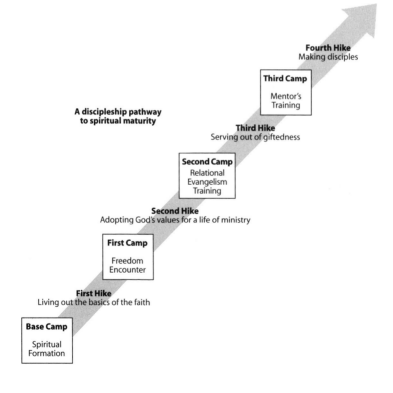

A discipleship pathway to spiritual maturity

Base Camp
Spiritual Formation

First Hike
Living out the basics of the faith

First Camp
Freedom Encounter

Second Hike
Adopting God's values for a life of ministry

Second Camp
Relational Evangelism Training

Third Hike
Serving out of giftedness

Third Camp
Mentor's Training

Fourth Hike
Making disciples

Base Camp – spiritual formation

An orientation meeting is vital to the success of the discipleship process. It brings everyone involved into a complete understanding of the process, what is expected, what to expect from one's mentor. It also helps the new disciple determine his or her point of origination. The lead pastor is present for the first part of the event to encourage and inspire the disciples and mentors, helping them see how God will powerfully use them and partner with them in building the kingdom. He will leverage his respected position to outline the measurable discipleship goals for the group. On behalf of the staff and church, he will commit all the church's resources to helping them become successful in their climb to achieve spiritual maturity.

The small group pastor is also present, and shares the importance of the biblical community in which the mentors and disciples belong. The disciples must clearly understand that their mentors will not be the sole relationship in the process. Other members of their groups will be there as a spiritual family to encourage, pray for, and spend time with them . The disciples learn that they should not place too much emphasis on their mentors alone and become overly dependent on one person. The mentors learn that their disciples will grow with their help as well as the input and relationships with others in their small groups. The message is clear: every child in the village has a parent, but the whole village takes responsibility for raising that child if they see an area in which they can be a positive influence.

Finally, the disciples take stock of where they are in their spiritual journeys and then they share this with their mentors (and small group leaders in the case of some of the churches I've surveyed). This is the most powerful part of the base camp. The disciples share how they came to a saving knowledge of Christ and when they were water baptized,[13] personal desires for spiritual and emotional growth, and their past as it pertains to religion or occult involvement or unhealthy relationships. (A self-assessment tool[14] is supplied to the disciples to help them know what and how much to share).

This spiritual formation gathering can be done in as little as three or four hours on a Saturday morning or a Sunday afternoon in a home or on the church campus. Most churches begin with one or two a year and then offer the event quarterly for all new believers who have come to Christ and are members of a small group. (Eventually, this event should be incorporated into the church's new-member process.)

The first hike – living out the basics of the faith:
"I write to you, children"

The first weeks in the mentor-disciple relationship are crucial. A relational rhythm must be developed (spending time together doing fun things, praying together, discussing the basics of the faith, truths from the Bible, and enjoying fellowship with other small group members). Most churches supply their mentors and disciples with a resource[15] covering foundational subjects such as listening to God, the sinful nature of man, the importance of the Bible, and developing basic spiritual disciplines (personal prayer and Bible reading).

The most successful disciple-making churches also help the disciples understand the damage caused by satanic strongholds to create a militant desire to find lasting freedom. By adding this component into the first days of discipleship, the new believers will quickly learn that confessing sin (a fruit issue) is good, and eradicating the source of the besetting sin even better! Nothing feels as good as being free from bitterness, resentment, anger, or anything else that Satan has used to defeat believers and break their spirits.

The first camp – experiencing freedom in Christ:
"I write to you, young men"

There is a strong correlation between successful discipleship and spiritual freedom from strongholds.[16] Those that discover their strongholds and work hard to find the roots early in their spiritual lives gain a strong sense of purpose and lose the cloud of shame that so often hangs over them. This kind of freedom helps them boldly share their faith with unchurched friends and embrace the powerful use of spiritual gifts. This is why it is vital that you provide a freedom encounter for your new disciples within two or three months of entering the discipleship path.

The most effective way to provide this experience is to reserve space in a retreat center away from the distractions of the city or town in which the disciple lives. Separate retreats for men and women seem to be the most common in churches I've researched. Same-sex retreats also solve the childcare issue and cuts lodging costs. The content of this retreat should cover the following basic areas:

- Previous involvement in false religions or the occult
- Destructive attitudes, habits, and actions (including addiction)
- Idolization of things or persons
- Rebellion against authority
- Word curses, vows, and judgments
- A lack of blessing from one's parents

A number of ministry resources are available so you don't have to recreate the wheel.[17] The issue is not which one to use, but how to use it. Your goal is to create a simple weekend event that allows disciples to learn about the damage strongholds cause and how to be set free of them through confession and the healing power of God. Avoid parachurch ministries whose goal is to develop a deliverance ministry that robs you of small group leaders in your church. People must be set free to minister to others with their biblical community, not build an outside organization's structure in your church that competes with purpose-driven life in biblical community.

Your first freedom encounter should be for those staff members, deacons, elders, and spouses who are currently in small groups. By moving through the process yourselves, you will be able to testify to its importance and share experiences of spiritual freedom in upcoming weekends.

With all this stated, I must say that one encounter weekend experience is not enough to become genuinely free from strongholds. I've been to a half dozen deliverance weekends as a disciple, a mentor, and then a facilitator. Each time, the Lord showed me another "layer of the onion" that required confession and a focused time of personal examination to find the root issues and receive God's healing. As you help people find the fruits and roots of their strongholds, stress that this will be a lifelong pursuit and requires the assistance of others. This is what Paul meant when he wrote, "work out your salvation with fear and trembling."[18]

The second hike – adopting God's values while discarding the values of this world

After the freedom weekend, the disciple may feel ten pounds lighter from all the confession, but the weight of the world returns quickly. His or her values are ungodly or a mixture of godly values and earthly values and require examination and radical change.

Old values are more easily discarded when new ones have been adopted and there is no room for the old. The mentor's level of patience is most important now. The disciple must see a life devoted to Christ and a way to adopt it. At this point in their relationship, the depth of maturity in the mentor will certainly be challenged. He or she cannot forcibly make the disciple discard old values for the new, but certainly should pray and fast for breakthroughs.

The disciple's small group plays an important role in the new believer's life at this point in his or her spiritual journey. The group members must show the new believer that a group of people can enjoy time together without drugs or alcohol. The group members also serve as a support for the mentor. And last but not least, the group members are part of the disciples' fishing team, befriending his or her unchurched friends to show them Christ's love.

To successfully move the disciple from the first camp to the second camp, I recommend you use one of any number of excellent resources available to help the disciple adopt new values.[19] The key here is to not overburden the mentor by asking him or her to teach the disciple beyond modeling; doing so risks mentor burnout or control issues. The disciple needs an easy-to-use resource that will help him or her wrestle with issues such as ethics, morality, avarice, debt, prioritizing ministry, balancing career and family, and tithing. By moving through a resource covering these tough areas, the mentor can ask the disciple questions and play the role of the "good cop."

The second camp – relational evangelism: "I write to you, fathers"

At this point, the disciple has found freedom from strongholds and is growing in the Lord. Learning how to "overlap" his or her friendships with the members of his biblical community is not only appropriate at this point but necessary for continued growth.

The sooner a disciple sees a friend come to Christ because of the radical changes that have taken place in his life, the easier it will be to stay on course and become a mentor.

Truthfully, excited new believers need very little training in relational evangelism. They just need to learn how to share the plan of salvation at the appropriate time. However, if your small groups are not increasing in size and number through relational evangelism, all of your group members should attend this camp the first time you hold it. This will serve as a kick-off for your mentor-based discipleship process. When a small group member sees a friend come to Christ because of her friendship and the relationship the convert has developed with other small group members, she will then become her friend's mentor and bring the friend to the spiritual formation seminar (base camp).

The content of this second camp must explain how people come to Christ through relational evangelism and contrast it with other methods the participants may have used in the past or were fearful they'd be required to use in relational evangelism. Like the freedom retreat, this should be a highly interactive event. The participants need time to share positive things about their unchurched friends with others from their small group in attendance, and discuss ways they can overlap their lives with each other's friends to see what may develop.[20]

You may discover that some or many of your small group members have no friends outside your congregation. For these people, the event should have a time for confession to others in their group, followed by a discussion of what they want to do differently to create new friendships with unchurched persons.

This camp does not have to be held at a retreat center, but it's powerful if you can swing it. Any time you can drag people away from

their world for a Friday night and Saturday you will find that participation increases and gives them a much-needed break from their
hectic lives. Most churches hold this event on a Saturday morning or
Sunday afternoon on the church campus, but there's no reason you
couldn't organize a large camping trip to make it fun for the kids too.

The third hike – serving out of giftedness

In many churches, members are urged to use their spiritual gifts
to support the organization. "Serving the Lord" translates into volunteering to help the pastoral staff get something done or fill a position in a program. In a church focused on developing fully devoted
believers through biblical community, the focus is on developing the
person into a powerful minister. Volunteering for vital ministries will
come naturally if you disciple people for their ministry to the world
and not to support the organization. In Philippians 3:14, Paul writes,
*"I press on toward the goal to win the prize for which God has called me
heavenward in Christ Jesus."* Even though he was imprisoned at the
time, I don't think his heavenward call was being a greeter in the first
service or teaching a junior high Sunday school class.

The current perception of spiritual gifts must change so the use
of them can shift radically and the way a person discovers them
changes as well. I love what Paul Ford says about spiritual gifts: "It is
not where you are good at something or comfortable, but rather
where you are powerful in the Spirit. It is not your natural skills or
strength. It is the dynamic power of God at work, first inside and
then outward from you to others."[21] Your goal is to help disciples see
where God is using them powerfully, which may not be comfortable
in the least bit!

To help disciples discover where they are powerful and not just

152

comfortable, use a spiritual gifts instrument based on observations made by other believers. Despite the wording in most instruments used today, a self-assessment will always be a reflection of what people want to do or where they are comfortable. I prefer to use gifts instruments (such as those designed by Paul Ford) that invite the small group to give feedback and testify as to how God has used the person in a powerful, transformational way.

When a believer uses his or her spiritual gifts powerfully—coupled with freedom from strongholds and an understanding of how to be a real friend to show the love of Christ to others naturally—the person possesses a profound clarity of purpose. The values and worldly priorities the person struggled to abandon become unimportant compared to living powerfully in Christ.

The third camp – becoming a mentor

A mentor's job is complete when his or her disciple has reached a friend for Christ and is successfully discipling the person. This half-day overview is to help maturing disciples adopt their new role as a spiritual parent for a new believer. The content includes practical information such as:

- Determining a time and place to meet with one's disciple
- Overcoming apprehension about discussing the relationship openly with the disciple to ensure the relationship remains effective
- Knowing when the mentor is being controlling or not supportive enough
- Establishing healthy boundaries (avoiding late-night calls, loaning money, and so forth.)

- Helping the disciple search for and self-disclose root issues of problems or issues
- Modeling a life of prayer and devotion to reading the Word
- Developing friendships with other members of the group that create a healthy family environment
- Making a commitment to move through the church's discipleship pathway again with the new believer

If a disciple reaches a friend for Christ before he or she is ready to mentor—which is determined on a case-by-case basis—the new believer should join the disciple when he or she meets with the mentor. As long as the first disciple is willing to take responsibility for the new believer and not place the entire relational and developmental load on the mentor, this will work out well and may be even more fulfilling for the mentor.

What's next?

While many churches have subsequent camps and hikes beyond mentor training, this will be the last one I explore. All the churches I've researched go in different directions at this point. Some take disciples into deeper studies of the Word or areas of spiritual maturity. Others move soul-winning mentors into small group leadership training or appoint them as group leaders and train them, knowing they will listen intently (like teaching someone to tread water or swim when they're drowning at the deep end of the pool). Your church must determine what is best for the disciple in the long run to provide a lifetime of ministry to others.

A team-based implementation strategy

Before I understood the developmental process behind a team-based implementation strategy, I wondered why so many churches failed to disciple people through mentoring. The case for a team-based strategy is so clear from Scripture. After all, these churches were not filled with brand new Christians who had yet to memorize Matthew 28:18-20. Like so many pastors, I remained puzzled. The small group members knew they were to make disciples, yet no one wanted to do it. There's a big difference between knowledge and desire.

Then it hit me like a ton of bricks. For generations, these members were spoon-fed from the pulpit and were considered pillars of the church if they tithed off their gross income and volunteered to serve on a committee or work with the youth. The bar was not only low, it was designed to recognize and even elevate those who made the organization run smoothly. It had little to nothing to do with taking responsibility for another person's spiritual maturity.

As I stated earlier, it's also difficult to envision yourself as a potential mentor when you've never been mentored. This is the most obvious roadblock you will encounter if you attempt to implement your relational discipleship pathway with a "let's get this done right away" mindset. What follows is a tried-and-true way of creating a discipleship pathway with a team, testing it to see if it produces what you hoped it would produce, and then modeling it for others so you can speak with authority and recent experience.

Assemble a team

There is no comparison between the results of one versus the results of a team. You must not attempt to design and implement a mentor-based discipleship pathway alone. This is a huge undertaking that is quite possibly a shift in lifestyle for everyone involved. Employ the "safety in numbers" principle and assemble an implementation team.

Gather a dozen faithful members of your small group ministry and invite them to your home. Share your urgency to see every member activated for a powerful and personal ministry to others outside the four walls of the church building. Reveal that the weekend services and small group participation don't produce fully devoted followers of Christ, but they do remain excellent support for true disciple-making. Then help them see the need for one-on-one discipleship by asking them if they've been mentored and what it achieved. (Interview each person invited to the meeting beforehand so you will not be surprised by what is or is not shared.) The goal of the evening is to cast the seed of discipleship to a group of potential team members to discover who is energized by the opportunity. The people that call you and tell you they are anxious to learn more are potential implementation team members. Choose the most strategic and practical people from that group and you have formed your team.

In the months to follow, meet with each one of them individually and together. When you are with them one-on-one each month, challenge them to spend more time with unchurched friends and employ the principles of relational evangelism. This may be a sizable challenge if they have no unchurched friends, but your time investment into each of them will be valuable. While together, discuss the ways you are investing time into building a friendship with an unchurched person. The goal for this stage of implementation is for the team members to win a friend to Christ sooner than later and become the first mentors.[22]

The first team meeting

When you meet with the team members for the first monthly team meeting, ask them to share what they think comprise the milestones and corresponding components of a discipleship pathway. Help them put the components in an order that creates a natural progression. Be sure to ask questions such as, "What will be the mentor's role in this part of the process?" "How will it look when the mentor's portion of the relationship is being done well?" This moves the team members to think like a mentor and take personal responsibility for the pathway's success. Finally, invest a sizable portion of your time praying together for an opportunity to disciple a new believer.

You may find that giving each person a brief research assignment in the first meeting heightens ownership. Ask one member to contact all the churches in a ten- or twenty-mile radius and ask the lead pastors about their discipleship pathway. Ask a couple others to contact other churches in your movement, stream, or denomination that are making disciples successfully. If they come back and say, "No one is making true disciples or doing anything outside the church building" they will be even more committed to making discipleship work in your church. If they return with information about someone else's successful relational discipleship path, they will validate your process or reveal weak areas in your pathway.

Your monthly meetings with the team should continue for at least six months. Use the time to review the plan of action, pray for unbelievers, and discuss the progress of the first mentoring partnerships.

Prototype it

Once your team has produced a pathway to spiritual maturity that everyone on the team (including you) thinks will create a fully devoted follower of Christ, you're ready to introduce it to no more than a half-dozen new Christians and the small group members who led them to Christ. Because this is a new process and possibly implemented in a completely new way, it is not wise to offer this to every group member that reaches a friend for Christ. Hand pick the ones who are of the same sex as the person reached and people who have a solid friendship. If a small group member reaches a coworker for Christ but that person has never met the others in the member's small group, this is not a good pair for the prototype phase. You are looking for new believers who have joined the group in which the potential mentor belongs.

When you find these established relationships, visit with the new believer, the potential mentor, and their group's leader. Explain that you want to see the disciple grow in all areas of life and become a fully devoted follower of Christ. Ask the potential mentor if he or she is willing to help the person grow spiritually by praying with him and meeting him over coffee once a week to talk about what he is learning. Then ask the leader if he or she will be supportive and check in with both of them and you.

As the lead pastor, your participation in the prototype phase is paramount to your success. Bring an unbelieving friend into relationship with your small group and then to Christ. Then walk the person through the discipleship pathway as a mentor. You must lead the way and model the life of a mentor for your church.

Refine it

As the first disciples are mentored through your church's pathway, the team will no doubt be presented with unforeseen issues. Before your monthly meetings, ask team members to interview a group leader, mentor, and disciple individually. Their goal with the interview is to find out what's working, what is not working well, and to listen carefully when those interviewed share ideas and opinions. When the team members report what they have found, it will cause them to think deeply about the required changes and they won't look to you for solutions.

Because so much process tweaking will be required, it is still not time to introduce your discipleship pathway to all new believers and mentors. Add a few more prototype mentors and disciples to test the changes the team has made. Do not rush to say it's "good enough" and publicize it. Making changes on the fly with people who don't like change will reduce their confidence in you, the team, and the discipleship process.

Prioritize it

While prototyping the discipleship path, you will quickly see how the camps and resource funding have impacted your church's calendar and budget. By moving into this slowly, you will have the time to prioritize discipleship over other programs in your church that should be supportive but not competitive. One area in which you will certainly make changes is in your men and women's ministries (if you have them). These are a perfect fit as a launching pad for mentoring in your small groups when the time is right. Scheduled retreats can be transitioned into freedom encounters. Gatherings should be geared toward how to disciple a person and be a better mentor.

The idea behind modifying existing ministries to be supportive of your mentor-assisted discipleship pathway is twofold. The first is that these ministries have calendar priority and have a spot in your church's budget. If you transition existing ministries, you have access to their time and resource allocations. The second reason is that you don't want competition for discipleship in your group. If a prime candidate for mentoring is heavily involved in the men's ministry, he may want to abandon his participation in that program to disciple a new believer in his small group.

Launching mentor-based discipleship through relational evangelism

Forming the team and creating the discipleship pathway will take time. Most churches with whom I've worked take a full year to research other churches and resources and to test a pathway to see if it produces fully devoted followers of Christ who want to mentor others. Invest this time to move your small group members into highly relational, outwardly focused people. If each of your small groups will reach just one or two people for Christ in the next three to six months, it will jump-start your new mentoring model of discipleship and bring them all up to speed at the right time.

Matchmaking mentors to altar converts

In many evangelical churches, a corporate gathering would not be complete without an altar call. One would think that assigning the new believer with a mentor at the altar or soon after would be a great move, but this violates two relational rules: the mentor did not lead the person to Christ through a genuine friendship and the new believer has no spiritual family or small group yet. Matchmaking new believers and mentors who are not friends fails consistently for a reason. The mentor-disciple association was externally created. For mentoring to work consistently in an equipping process, multiple points of relational connection between the mentor and disciple must exist. The more hobbies, interests, and relationships the two have enjoyed together prior to conversion, the greater the rate of success.

Instead of matchmaking mentors to converts, work overtime to help converts find a small group and become a functional part of that spiritual family. Encourage leaders to involve the new converts in hosting the small group in their homes and serving the other members as soon as possible. Giving as much as one receives is a key to attracting new friends and cultivating a relationship with a potential mentor.[23] When the new believer is viewed as a new servant in the group, it's the right time for the leader to see natural connections between the new believer and more mature members for discipleship.

In all honesty, I do not prefer this strategy. If a church must use it frequently, it shows that the conversions are coming from a pulpit-centered model. I do realize that it must be used though, especially when families who move into the neighborhood show up on Sunday morning and have no established friendships. So use it sparingly and closely monitor the conversion growth in your church to make sure a majority is derived through relational evangelism.

Moving inward groups outward

Are your small group members on fire for Christ and reaching friends left and right? You're good to go. Skip this section and implement your discipleship path. On the other hand, if your small groups are filled with God-loving people who soil themselves when they hear the word evangelism, this section is for you and you desperately need what I'm about to share with you.[24]

One of my favorite relational evangelism tools for small groups is a poster called *The Blessing List*.[25] There's nothing special about it. It's just a big piece of paper with blank lines on it. But it's a very powerful instrument for outreach when properly used. The poster unfolds and is placed conspicuously on a wall in the room where the group will gather and is kept by the host to ensure it goes up each time the group meets. At the first few meetings, members place the first names of unchurched friends on the list. As each name is written on the list, the members share one or two things they love about the person. Each member is challenged to brag about the person and refrain from sharing anything the member would not say if the person were in the room. The list can be taken down if a friend comes to the group, and a new list can be created so the new pre-Christian member of the group can add a name or two and share why they love those friends so much.

The idea behind a *Blessing List* is not to treat those on it as if they were "God's most wanted" or "on God's hit list." After all, who'd want to get to know someone that is characterized as a screwed-up individual with a bad temper, drinking habit, addiction, or some other character flaw? (Sharing why the person needs Christ so badly—which is gossip by anyone's definition—defeats the purpose of this list and drives others away from a desire to connect with them in friendship.) Each week the leader draws attention to the list and invites members to share additional positive things about those on the list. He or she asks questions such as, "What hobbies are they involved with? What are their current interests? How long has the person been your friend? Why would it be cool for others in this group to get to know this person?"

The Blessing List keeps the group focused on outsiders for a portion of their gathering. By sharing positive things about the person and then praying that God would bless their socks off the next week, the members will soon see friendship connections if they're looking for them.

If you have some sort of aversion to using a poster like this one in your groups, you must find a different way to help your small group members see the harvest field that is all around them. They need to be shown that the word evangelism can be redefined in a very positive way and is synonymous with the word fun if it's done right.

The roles of the leader and coach

For a group to become outward-focused, the leader must become a motivator. He must challenge the group members to get to know each other's friends based on a common interest or hobby. When the members see what could be if they would embrace God's relational provision, the leader's role changes. He then focuses on scheduling activities and gatherings at which unchurched friends of members can gather and mingle.

In my role as a coach, I ask each leader about the group's outreach plans each time we meet one-on-one. When I visit a group, I ask them to share with me their plans for relational outreach. On occasion, the only response I receive is blank stares or a total loss of eye contact. When this happens, I urge them to reach out and harness the power of their community to cross-pollinate with unchurched people or risk losing what they've worked so hard to achieve. Biblical community is like manna. It must be used to fuel God's people to keep moving and extend his kingdom to others or it spoils.

Becoming attractive to others

Shifting the focus in your small groups from inward to outward will not take place overnight. A *Blessing List* on the wall will keep outreach in front of them each time the group meets, but the small group members must be attractive as friends for the list to work. When Christians are not growing in one or more areas of their lives (especially in their walks with Christ) and are not a genuinely happy and joyful people, unbelievers will not be drawn to them or their group.

Here's a list of what I find attractive in a new friend. The person I will most readily befriend . . .

- is working hard at accomplishing goals in his or her life
- has taken ownership for his past actions and current condition or situation
- is actively pursuing a hobby, sport, more education, or an activity, or is passionate about something that is non-work related (even if I am not immediately interested in it)
- works hard at work and plays hard at play
- enjoys new foods and cultural experiences
- maintains a positive outlook
- is not content with the same routine
- places a higher value on people than possessions
- enjoys being around me when I am serious or silly

If small group members have no friendships with unchurched persons, there's a high likelihood they are not relationally attractive. When asked about their weekend on Monday morning, they tell coworkers about doing chores around the house or going to a Little League game on Saturday and then "going to church" on Sunday. If they share that they are heavily involved in a church program that is designed to serve others in the subculture, it communicates their entrenchment in an organization with which the unchurched person cannot identify.

Your first step is to challenge the members to ask, "What is attractive about my walk with Christ, my lifestyle, my outlook on life, my goals and dreams, and my general demeanor? Do others perceive me as a narrow-minded religious person who is happy to live in a religious subculture without any interest in the world around me? In what ways do I relate to others who have wildly different opinions about spirituality, lifestyle, or goals and dreams for their lives?"

Get this right and avoid shortcuts!

When your small group members develop genuine friendships with unchurched persons, everything changes for them and a new purpose in life emerges. They will see Christ working powerfully through them in their actions and reactions to things that their unchurched friends say and do. Sharing their lives with unbelievers shapes Christians and prepares them to mentor in a way that no classroom can provide. The relationships give them a natural desire to take responsibility for the new Christians and become their spiritual parents.

Whatever you do, don't take shortcuts. Let's review the principles covered in this chapter:

- Develop a relational discipleship path with a team.
- Prototype it for as long as it takes to produce disciple makers.
- When it has been refined, implement it with small group members who have reached a friend for Christ and brought that new believer into their biblical community.

- Provide immersion events (such as spiritual formation, spiritual freedom, and spiritual gifts weekends) to give the disciple a sense of connection to the larger church body and lighten the load for the mentor.
- Invite the first mentors and disciples to give you feedback as to how to better serve them, and be willing to change anything that is not working well.

Relational discipleship is not an option

Jesus modeled a relational, holistic, one-to-one discipleship process that changed the world. His disciples lived in a Christ-centered community where they learned what it meant to walk out their knowledge of God and God's ways. By watching Jesus and ministering with him, they learned how to treat others gently, handle money, walk in purity, interpret Scripture, pray fervently, heal the sick, and lead from a place of submission to their Authority.

If you want your small group ministry to be the church in action and to be transformational for every member of every group, you must replicate what Jesus provided the disciples (and what they provided for many others). It is not enough to provide a sermon series and urge them to attend a small group meeting. There must be life-on-life interaction, turning members into soul-winning mentors.

Let me close this chapter with a quote from a man I highly respect. Dennis Watson is the lead pastor of a successful disciple-making small-group-based church in a suburb of New Orleans. He has this to say about the importance of relational discipleship:

Our cell groups are great tools for discipleship purposes because they provide modeling and mentoring for discipleship as well as teaching discipleship. However, our cell ministry is only successful because it includes a strategy for member-to-member discipleship.

It is my belief that every person needs a "Paul" and "Barnabas" in their life if they are to truly become fully devoted followers of Jesus. Every person needs someone they are mentoring and someone who is mentoring them if they are to experience true discipleship and fulfill the goals and purposes of what cell ministry is all about.[26] ◆

CHAPTER FIVE

The naked truth about small group leadership: it's time to break with tradition

Each time I find the opportunity, I ask small group leaders if they are developing an apprentice. Only one out of twenty American small group leaders I have interviewed when visiting churches can name a person in their group who has publicly committed to leadership. In the West, only a fraction of small group members envision themselves as future small group leaders. Even if their biblical community has been the most transformational thing they've ever experienced, they are unwilling to help others enter into it by leading a group.

Applying what I covered in the last chapter will certainly mobilize members to reach friends for Christ and disciple them, which makes them "leaders of one." From this vantage point, leading a group should be a natural progression. Discipling a friend at a coffee shop is easy. Preparing for meetings every week, keeping up with a dozen people, attending leader's meetings, and meeting with a coach is far more time-intensive and daunting. As good as mentoring is, it does not always produce someone who is eager to lead a group at the very moment you desperately need a leader.

Who's in charge of finding and developing new leaders?

Traditional thinking maintains that the existing leader of a group is responsible to develop an apprentice who will take over the group or leave to start a new group in twelve to fourteen months. Ideally, the training process should take approximately six months if the leader gives the apprentice responsibility and the person takes it and runs with it:

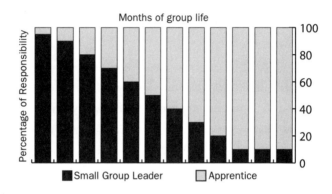

This strategy sounded great when I read it years ago in resources written by Yonggi Cho, Carl George, Dale Galloway, and my father, Ralph Neighbour, Jr. My wife and I formed groups throughout the 1990s using this strategy and I taught it hundreds of times in seminars and workshops. When I showed the illustration above to a group of small group leaders, I shared my personal goal for development: to shape my apprentice into a servant, knowing that the members of my group would follow someone who selflessly served them.

Of course, as a small group leader I was not alone in the training of my apprentice. My church supplemented my mentoring with a training class covering the stages of group life (forming, storming, norming, performing, reforming); how to deal with EGRs (Extra Grace Required persons who won't shut up in meetings or won't share anything beyond their thoughts on the weather); how to limit damage from MCIs (those with a Multiple Critter Infestation); group agenda design (creating observation, interpretation, and application questions from a Bible passage); and so on. The combination of the mentoring and training apprentices was the only way we knew how to expand our groups, so we worked that system hard. When my church had both of these elements working flawlessly, a new leader was developed in less than a year and he or she was both confident and competent to lead.

In the traditional model, leader burnout is very low if the new group is launched with both a leader and an apprentice. This keeps the leader from carrying the entire burden of leadership and it contains a bonus feature: the group has a new leader for multiplication as it grows.

Whom am I kidding?

In all my years of small group leadership, my wife and I have started only one group with an apprentice. The others have been launched with people who desired community but did not view themselves as future small group leaders. As these groups grew in size, I developed one of the members to take over the group with covert methods. This worked for the most part but was anything but ideal because it backfired now and then. However, it did work more than it failed so it's worth sharing (see the sidebar on the following page).

Member complacency

If the small group leader and apprentice are doing an amazing job of ministering to the members and facilitating meetings, the members need not worry about anything beyond supplying snacks or hosting the meetings in their homes. If the members do any more

Covert Ops

My strategy for leadership development when I found myself without an apprentice was downright sneaky. I asked various members for favors—pray with a needy member of the group, facilitate a meeting when I was out of town, or spearhead a service project—until I found one that followed through consistently. Over time, I asked this person to do many different things for the group members but not more than one thing at a time so as not to make the person feel overwhelmed or abused.

At some point, I invited the person to come to a leadership meeting as my special guest. I thought that if the person showed up and enjoyed the time with our small group pastor, he or she would walk into my carefully crafted leadership trap. If I developed enough of a genuine friendship with the member, the person usually agreed.

When I was confident the person had very little wiggle room to reject the offer of small group leadership, I invited him to lunch (conveniently forgetting to inform the person that our small group pastor would be joining us). During our meal, my pastor would then encourage the person to enroll in leadership training and move into my role because the church had other plans for me. More than half the time, the member agreed to take over the group. After all, he'd done most of the things a leader does without knowing he was being trained.

As I stated, covert leadership development strategies like this have merit, but this method is ripe for failure. If a member doesn't volunteer to help in all the ways needed to make a confident commitment, the group and the leader are stuck. Despite our best efforts, my wife and I led one group for two years without an apprentice.

172

for the group, they consider themselves helpful volunteers (and by now you know why I'm not a fan of volunteerism). The upside? The leader-apprentice model makes joining a group easy. The downsides are low ownership and high complacency, which trump the "easy-in" feature every time.

The diagram below shows how many small group leaders and members perceive their level of responsibility for the group's success:

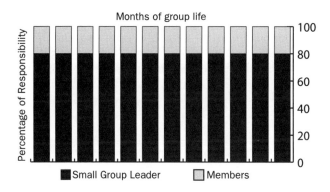

Take note that this diagram shows *perception*, not reality. Even if the members are pitching in when they see a need or they're asked to help, the leader may *feel* completely responsible for member maturity and group health and expansion, leading to stress and burnout.

The weight of leadership

As a leader, I never thought about the amount of responsibility placed upon me by my pastor. I eagerly agreed to relate to and be-friend a dozen people, orchestrate a weekly gathering, develop a set of powerful questions from a Bible passage or the pastor's sermon each week, and be the first person my members called in times of calamity.

On top of all this, I worked hard to develop and release a new leader from my group every year or so. I know full-time pastors who struggle to do this! Why on earth was my church placing this much responsibility on a guy with a family, a career, and a perennial honey-do list?

When I moved into a coaching role over groups, the burden of leadership became abundantly clear. My leaders fully understood their role and worked overtime to fulfill it. Yet most were unable to find and train a member to take over their group. It was all they could do to love and serve the members of their group and ensure the meetings went smoothly. The stress of leading alone and knowing it should be different created an unfair sense of inadequacy. These were excellent leaders who simply did not have members with a stake in the group's success or failure.

How are you training your leaders?

The typical small group leader-training process includes teaching on group dynamics, meeting flow, and basic leadership principles. Some churches cover these topics over a six- or eight-week period while others cover all the material on a Saturday crash course on leading a group. One could argue that the first method is superior because it disseminates the needed information in smaller doses over time, increasing retention. Neither is worthy of dialog. Both methods are an information dump for the future leader. A better argument would be to step back and challenge the teaching model, not how it is delivered.

My dad taught me a bunch of things growing up, most of which I didn't value because I didn't have a use for them at the time. One of those things was an understanding of how people successfully adopt new values and make radical changes in their lifestyle. Today I greatly value this information. It explains the ineffectiveness of so much of the small group leader training found in churches today. New leaders are supplied with knowledge about how to lead a small group, but few have been given the time and opportunity to learn through trial and error before leading a group.

Knowledge is not transformational unless it is applied in the form of a new habit that changes a person's lifestyle. Following is a brief explanation of the three domains of learning. As you read the descriptions, consider your leadership training process. Ask yourself if your training moves your future leaders through all three domains in each area of leadership prior to taking a group.

The Cognitive Domain

This basic domain of learning is characterized by sharing knowledge verbally or in written form in the hope the recipient will retain the new information. A vast majority of the teaching and training we receive in the church today is based on the cognitive learning model. Someone stands up and talks and we are encouraged to listen intently, take notes, and apply what is being shared. Or, we're given a book to read and we're challenged to apply what we're reading.

The cognitive approach isn't an effective training method by itself. A single Saturday leadership training model delivers a shotgun blast of cognitive information to leaders that typically goes in one ear and out the other. There's simply too much information being supplied at one time without the benefit of the other domains of learning. At best, the person attending a one-day seminar will gain enough information to be dangerous.

The Psychomotor Domain

The psychomotor domain is characterized by learning through action. A deeper understanding is gained when a person participates in a new activity versus just hearing or reading about it. For example, taking a member with you to pray with another member in the group is a psychomotor activity. The activity helps the potential leader fully understand the power behind a prayer visit, described earlier in a cognitive training session. Many small group leader-training resources can be made far more effective if the principles taught are combined with exercises that must be completed prior to moving on to the next section. Cognitive information becomes valuable when its put to use and a positive outcome is produced.

Here is where many pastors using a six- or eight-week training approach are deceived. They have trained members to facilitate group meetings and assigned tasks to solidify leadership practices. Because the members have successfully completed their homework assignments, the pastor assumes he's produced a leader when in fact he's produced a member who has toyed with leadership tasks. This may give the member some confidence, but little competence, to take a group. The member must move into another domain to become a proficient and passionate small group leader.

The Affective Domain

Moving into the affective domain is characterized by a shift in lifestyle or behavior. The knowledge is no longer theoretical (cognitive information) or a best practice (psychomotor activity). The person who has moved into the affective domain has adopted a new set of values that drives his decision-making. Three signs that measure a potential leader's arrival into the affective domain are:

176

1. The person has discarded old patterns of selfishness to serve others and now views the group and its members like a servant leader, not a consuming member.
2. The person has become a self-feeder (reading books about small group leadership on her own; visiting other groups to learn; signing up for additional training courses without being urged to do so).
3. The person has developed a strategic mindset and approach concerning the growth of the group as a whole and each member individually.

I've not found many churches in America that take the time and energy to develop leaders to this depth before they are given groups. Most small group pastors train at the cognitive level and hope for the best. They don't have the time to move potential leaders deeper into psychomotor activity. Only a fraction of those that give potential leaders homework assignments follow up with each person to ensure they are learning through experience. The pressure is on most small group pastors to produce leaders for enfolding new congregational members, not transformed individuals who have a missional heart and hunger to lead a small group of believers to expand the kingdom.

What are you training your leaders to be?

The small group meeting is the most public part of a leader's ministry, but not the most important. Focusing on meeting components at the expense of the far more powerful relational aspects of leadership makes the role mechanical and labored.

During training events in local churches, I'm consistently approached by small group leaders who say, "I'm doing everything I was taught to do during my meetings and my group isn't growing. What am I missing?" Of course, when I ask them how often they spend time with members having fun, talking, praying, and serving others together, the persons loses eye contact and replies, "I know I should do more of that but I just don't have time. The best I can do is prepare for the meetings each week."

When I train leaders, my desire to produce a good meeting facilitator is overshadowed by a hunger to see them become a servant and friend to their fellow small group members. When potential leaders are trained to focus on people instead of meetings, the formal gatherings take care of themselves and quell the fear of inadequacy.

Two or three times a month, Etna and I cook a meal for our closest friends. On more than one occasion, the meals we've served were undercooked or poorly prepared. I distinctly remember grilling rib eye steaks to the consistency of shoe leather. Yet our friends keep coming back for dinner. Our interest and care for one another is far deeper than our ability to serve the perfect gourmet meal. One of our friends (a guy who was a small group member in our last group) helped us decorate our living room and found the perfect artwork and a rug. Another friend asked me to work on her computer. Then she helped me create handmade invitations for Etna's birthday party.

It's no different with effective small group leaders. I know of a couple who have multiplied their small group repeatedly through the years with new believers and new leaders. When I visited their small group, their facilitation skills were anything but stellar. Despite this, they loved being with their group members and it showed. The relational lifestyle of the leaders with group members made the meetings wonderful. They enjoyed meals together, served one another, prayed together regularly, and cross-pollinated these friendships with unchurched friends. All this happened outside of the weekly meeting. Successful meetings are not a goal, but a result of doing life together. The relationships with one another and Christ (a genuine biblical community) are the driving force for these successful small group leaders.

Transformational friendships

Ask any group of people which they'd rather do: attend a well-designed church meeting or spend time with a friend. The friend will win every time. If you strip away all the formal responsibilities of a good small group leader, friendship with Christ, group members, and future group members is the foundation built under their ministry.

Most small group leader training I've reviewed or used—including the material my own ministry currently offers—is well rounded and addresses the relational aspects of small group leadership. The issue is not with the content, but the relationship—or lack thereof—between the student and the teacher. Are you a friend to your potential leaders? Do you spend enough time with them to discover their capacity to relate to others as a genuine friend? It's not enough to tell them that friendship is important and to focus on the members of the group between meetings. This is a cognitive exchange of information. What the future leader needs is to practice building successful friendships with other group members to move them into psychomotor activity. If they don't naturally do it, they must be mentored by their leader, their coach, and by you as their lead trainer.

Moving people into group leadership who have not developed deep friendships with others in their group is a waste of everyone's time. If the person is not the kind of friend that lays his or her life down for others, the group will struggle to become a spiritual family that matures and produces fruit. No amount of training in the area of meeting facilitation is going to make a group successful if the leader is not shown how to lead relationally.

Establishing self-motivating leadership

Developing relationship-driven small group leaders requires a life-changing training process. In most cases, the transformation from member to leader takes months (not weeks or hours) of one-on-one mentoring by the trainer, the leader's future coach, and the group leader serving the potential leader. Take a critical look at your training process with the following in mind: Does it effectively move the potential leader through all three domains of learning? Do the participants receive enough time and energy from you to catch a vision for relational ministry and then live it out? Do your coaches and existing leaders carry their weight of the relational and mentoring aspects of leadership development? Is your training process heavily weighted on building transformational relationships with others instead of facilitation skills and meeting dynamics?

The church that releases leaders based on their training attendance instead of their lifestyle will create a meeting-focused small group ministry. If you find your leaders invest a majority of their time and energy on meeting preparation, you should overhaul your training process. Produce leaders who have followers, not acquaintances who show up for weekly meetings.

Self-Assessment

In Chapter 4, I discussed the power of self-assessment to create a point of origination. Encouraging a small group member to earn a leadership position requires a continuation of the same self-assessment process. Most small group training resources are missing this foundational tool. Using a simple evaluation tool (such as the sample found in Appendix C) will raise ownership, set a standard, create a pathway for the future leader … and help you determine who is genuinely ready for a leadership position in your relational ministry.

The goal of a self-assessment tool is not to berate potential leaders for what they have not accomplished, but to help them see areas of ministry that require additional experience. Another aspect of a written self-assessment is the way it turns the small group pastor into the "good cop" and the assessment itself into the challenging "bad cop." If a small group pastor meets with a potential leader to review the results of the self-assessment, he or she has the opportunity to say, "You've got growth areas where I can be of great help to you. Choose one you want to work on and I will help you grow in that area."

It's all about the relationships

If the disciples had been selected for rabbinical school, they would have learned the proper way to perform highly religious practices for temple gatherings. Rabbis were also taught to avoid spending time with "unclean persons." Jesus changed all that. He illustrated the importance of spending time with the good, the bad, and the ugly as the lifestyle of a Christian leader. Jesus exposed his disciples to public teaching times as well, but a majority of what is written in the gospels surrounds his mentoring in the area of relationship-building while walking on the road, sitting by the shore, and relaxing in homes.

Instilling relational values in your new leaders to move them away from a meeting mentality is not difficult. It just takes a new paradigm for the lifestyle of a healthy small group leader. When you've fully adopted a relational paradigm for small group leadership, your development process will change, as will the quality of the leaders you produce. Will it take more time to train leaders? Yup. Will it produce healthier groups that need very little in the way of maintenance? Absolutely.

This is a good swap. Trust me.

What to do about it

Many areas of small group ministry are beyond the control of the small group pastor. Leaders or coaches move to another city for work with six week's notice, leaving a leadership gap. The small group ministry budget is cut to the bone and the annual leadership retreat must be cancelled. Or, five new families join the church in a matter of weeks and none of the groups are ready to multiply. The stress on the small group ministry and its pastor can be greatly diminished by maintaining a leadership pool of members who are ready and willing to lead.

I have no doubt you have thought about this before. A batch of leaders in the wings is a pipe dream for most pastors. At the expense of sounding as if I'm trying to sell you a new car, let me ask you a question: if I were to share a new paradigm for small group leadership development that produced highly relational candidates, would you be interested?

I thought so. Keep reading to learn how to develop healthier groups and leaders-o-plenty.

> *If it ain't broke...*
> If your church is using the leader-apprentice model and it is producing enough leaders for new groups, don't attempt to fix what's not broken. You may want to focus on what you are training your leaders to do or how you are training them and keep your small group leadership model intact. What follows is a new model for small group ministry leadership and membership. As you will see, it changes the way a member participates, a leader facilitates, a coach supports, and the small group pastor relates to everyone involved.

Turning members into core team members

Two years ago, the small group pastors at my church invited our group leaders to abandon their traditional leader-apprentice roles for something better. The motivation behind the shift was to eliminate burnout and ensure each group produced new leaders for group expansion.

Though I'd never seen it in action, I was more than happy to abandon the old way for something that actually turned members into leaders. Like most churches in America, my church was starved for new leaders. Too few of our group members had the courage to step into the role of the apprentice before or after a new group started. Our leaders were constantly looking for volunteers from their groups to help in one way or another, which was exhausting. My greatest concern was that ownership among members remained too low to move them into a leadership role. Our church was ripe for change.

Core teams: an overview

The concept behind this model is frightfully simple: involve every willing member in the planning and execution of those plans for prayer, evangelism, fellowship, servanthood, and meeting-related roles. Instead of the leader carrying the load, a core team of members in the group share responsibility as co-leaders. The diagram below shows a strong sense of ownership and activity the members carry in a core team-led group:

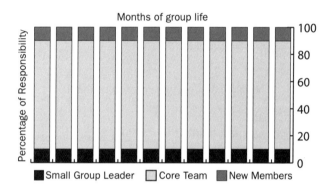

The new members do not initially feel a sense of responsibility and ownership in the group, which is quickly remedied. After just a few weeks, the person will be asked to serve the group in increasing ways. If the person becomes a servant, he or she is invited to join the core team.

The leader

The leader remains a vital component to the group's success. In this model, he or she acts as a group liaison, notifying church leadership of the team's vision and mission (direction and activities). The leader acts more like a representative and spokesperson for the team.

As you will see, the role is less dominant compared to the traditional model of leadership.

Type A personalities (take-charge, more aggressive people) are standouts for group leadership in the leader-apprentice model. They're willing to get the job done, even if it means tackling a project alone. Strong personalities will find the core team model challenging. To succeed, they must become a thoughtful team leader who facilitates by asking questions without pushing a personal agenda. The core team model opens up leadership for all the Type B personalities (easy-going, more passsive people) who have previously lived in the shadows. In fact, a warm, thoughtful, and quiet personality makes a *better* core team leader than a commanding, outgoing personality.

For example, the young adults that lead my group are the most laid-back, Type B individuals I've encountered. Megan is a gentle free spirit who loves to go with the flow. She is easy to be around and bubbly in personality. James is a natural team leader as well. He has no desire to control anything or anyone. He is often quiet until prompted to respond. Before Megan and James formed a core team, the group members possessed little visible ownership. Additionally, the leader's personalities were too passive for a traditional leadership role. We had twenty-five fringe members of the group, but our meetings consisted of nine or ten inconsistent individuals.

Everything changed when Megan and James formed a core team. For a number of months, I served on my group's core team to learn about it and help my group grow. Instead of delegating previously de-termined tasks to various people, Megan and James showed up without an agenda. We sat around looking at each other quietly that first night, but it sent a clear message. The members on the newly formed core team were responsible for the group's success, not just our fearless leaders.

We hit the ground running at our second meeting. Each of us showed up with creative ideas for our meetings, fun things to do together on weekends, and how our group could serve both our community and our church. I offered to be the outreach captain, inviting the team to think about how to turn an upcoming group barbecue into a social connection event to meet one another's unchurched friends.

You might be thinking this is how a traditional model of small group leadership *should* operate, and you'd be right. But it doesn't. Leaders grow weary of asking members to volunteer to do things in meetings and for the group. If the leader forgets or becomes too busy to ask others for help, he or she ends up doing everything for the group, resulting in burnout. The core team approach removes the burden of responsibility from the leader. When the members of the core team work together, it doesn't feel like a burden at all. In fact, it gives the members a clear and guiding purpose for membership and becomes a joy!

Two years ago, Shawn Barr introduced core team leadership to the small groups at Calvary Chapel, Melbourne, Florida. His desire was to revitalize their small groups and enable the ministry to grow organically. Serving as the church's new small group pastor, he prototyped core team leadership for six months with one of his groups. When the lead pastor saw the difference it made in the group, he encouraged Shawn to transition more groups. Recently, Shawn sent me an update on what this shift has done for each level of his church's small group ministry:

There have been several benefits from transitioning our home groups from a leader/apprentice model to core teams…

For the group members: We have seen more of our home

group members move from being takers (I'm here to be served) to givers (I am here to serve); we have seen an increase in the average attendance of a typical home group meeting (ownership); we have a larger percentage of our members actually taking leadership roles in the home group ministry (the stigma and expectation of having to lead a future group is now reduced because everyone is serving, not just the future leader).

For the small group leader: We have had less "leader burnout" and fewer groups close their doors; our leaders are now focused on doing ministry and are not caught up in the details of home group meetings.

For the small group coach: We have a larger pool from which to find future leaders. Our coaches now clearly see the potential for new groups to form.

For me, the small group pastor: I find that people have different reasons and objectives for home group participation. My focus is that each of our groups experience the indwelling Christ in their home group meeting, and that the meeting is not just a religious exercise. Knowing a core group is planning to focus each meeting on the presence, power, and purpose of Christ gives me assurance that the gathering will be a life-changing encounter with the Savior, regardless of each person's initial reasons for participation.[1]

The reason I'm so gung-ho on core team leadership is that it turns consumer members into responsible, productive, and motivated "pre-leaders." They are no longer volunteering to help their leader or an organization. They have become a shareholder in their group's success.

Core team formation

In new groups, every member is asked to serve as a core team member. Groups that are launched with a core team enjoy a strong start, remain mission-driven, and produce future leaders. Gone are the days of launching a group with two or three people who struggle for months to build momentum. Sending out six or seven people from an existing group to be the core team for a group plant gives the new group and the new leader strength in numbers and a missional mindset.

In established groups, the way to implement a core team approach is for the group's leader and coach or pastor to visit with each regularly attending member privately, inviting the person to be a part of a new core team. While most members will show interest, there will always be a subset of the group who are motivated enough to show up to the core team meetings. By inviting everyone, no one's feelings are hurt when plans are made without their direct input. (Approximately half of a group will have a strong interest in being a core team member. The other half is satisfied they were asked and know they can join at any time when they are ready.)

Core team particulars

The team creates plans to successfully live out the mission of the group, decides who will do what in upcoming meetings, organizes outreach events, and discusses when the group will be ready to branch or multiply.

What does the leader do? The leader facilitates the core team meetings. Most importantly, the leader refocuses his or her time to support mentor-driven discipleship.

What does the existing apprentice do? At first the apprentice is enrolled as an assistant to the leader and co-leads core team meetings in an increasing capacity toward the group's multiplication. If the group does not have an apprentice, the leader asks a core team member to serve as his or her assistant after two or three months to move a member into the position (with or without the title).

How often do core teams meet and how long are meetings? Core teams meet just once a month for approximately ninety minutes. Some teams get right to business and are done in an hour. Other teams take two hours because they enjoy one another's company and create plans over a meal. Ultimately, each core team must determine the meeting duration and frequency. It's all about results! Some core teams meet quarterly because the leader and core team members are very relational and spend a lot of free time together and planning is more ad hoc versus structured. Others need a monthly meeting because the members are not as relational.

Where do core teams meet? Anywhere they like. Some meet in a member's home so their kids can play while they plan; others gather at a restaurant or a coffee shop after a weekend service.

Core team meetings

In a typical core team gathering, the members begin with prayer. They petition God for a deeper understanding of what they should plan for during the meeting and for a heightened sense of direction as a group. This is followed by a time of intercession for each member of the group and members' unbelieving friends.

After prayer, the core team discusses the results of last month's plans and makes new plans for the next six weeks of group life. (By planning for six weeks instead of just four, the core team has enough overlap to make changes midstream or delay a core team meeting by a week if a holiday or a flu outbreak postpones a meeting.) During the planning part of the meeting, the leader helps the core team "think outside the room" as it pertains to involving future core team members in serving the group. The goal is to give every member of the group responsibility for its success. Even a hurting person should be employed to bring snacks, show up early to a meeting and vacuum the floors, or organize a community service project for the group with others.

New members who want to join the core team are always welcome. While larger planning teams will take longer to make decisions, increasing the size of the core team just before the group multiplies helps the team see the opportunity for two strong teams to emerge. The larger core team can easily be formed into two teams who meet together to pray and then separate to plan unique meetings or events.

Another meeting?

The only potential downside to a team-based leadership model is the need for another meeting. That's why it's a good idea to make changes in other areas of the small group ministry to offset the extra time investment.

If your church has monthly meetings for group leaders, reduce the number to four times a year and rebrand the event as a quarterly "core team rally." This event will be far larger and have more energy than a leader's gathering if you do it right. When you gather the team members, lead them to pray aloud for opportunities to share Christ with friends through relationships with other group members. Encourage them with testimonies of salvation and healing from within the small groups. Then, give them time to make plans for the next month of group life so they don't need to meet that month. This will take the place of their core team gathering for that month, and planning with other groups in the same room brings a renewed energy to the planning process.

One of the small groups I coach utilizes the fifth week in a given month to have the core team meeting instead of the actual small group gathering. They involve everyone in the planning and invite the members to come to the core team meetings if they have interest in serving the group in a greater capacity. By meeting at these times, it further reduces the number of additional meetings for the members of the core team.

Interaction with the Coach

As a small group coach, my role is far easier with core teams. I pop in on a core team meeting whenever I am able to do so. In fact, my wife and I invite each core team in our cluster to hold one of their planning meetings in our home each quarter. We serve store-bought lasagna and "salad in a bag," asking each team member to chip in five dollars to cover the cost of the meal. As they eat, we listen to the plans they are making and watch for the members who are taking the lead. Those are the future leaders of new groups.

Joining a group's core team planning session does not eliminate the one-on-one time I spend with the group's leader, but it has replaced some of the actual group visits I make. I glean far more about the group's health by listening to members make plans and discuss what is working or needs work in their group.

In years past, I was trained to view every small group member as a potential leader. Today I don't think this way. I've met small group members who should never become conventional group leaders because of their gift set. On the flip side, I've yet to meet a small group member who would not make an excellent core team member.

Interaction with the small group pastor

The pastor over groups will find that the time spent counseling burned-out leaders or scrambling to replace leaders will be greatly reduced. Visiting core team gatherings to cast vision may be required, but the pastor does not need to be present for the entire meeting. Leader meetings remain important, but core team gatherings become a new place of connection for the small group pastor.

This shift is not an increase or decrease in time use, but a change in mindset. Instead of primarily relating to leaders, the pastor relates with core team members. Much of the small group leader preparation is now done on the job as a core team member.

Turning core team members into leaders

The core team approach naturally moves a number of a group's members into the role of co-leader. Inviting one of the members to take a few of his or her fellow core team members and start a new group is not nearly as scary as asking the same person to become a leader of a new group and recruit volunteers to get things done.

The key to success is helping a core team embrace the lifestyle of a healthy biblical community. If a core team executes plans for powerful small group gatherings and effective outreach, the group will grow numerically. Numeric growth leads to a larger core team, and subgroups of the team are formed to strategize events. The subgroup team leaders become future group leaders when they have proven they have what it takes to get things done with a team.

The value of relational intimacy and missional living must be kept as a guiding foundation for small group involvement. By inviting core teams to talk about increasing the level of member intimacy and maintain it by launching a new group when they meet, it will become abundantly clear that branching is the key. Members who are new to group life always have a hard time with multiplication because they've never experienced life in community before. If their small group involvement has been that of a consumer or the goal of the group is fellowship, they will resist multiplication, even if a new leader is ready to go. Moving members into strategic planning and prayer for outreach and growth creates a hunger to "leave and cleave" to maintain forward momentum.

Graduating from membership to leadership

Core team members view leadership in a completely different way than a traditional small group member sees the role. Leaving the group with four or five others who have agreed to pray, plan, and execute plans for group life and outreach is not a leap. It's just the next step.

When I graduated from the eighth grade, I recall the fear of going to a new school with much older kids at the end of the summer break. I was certain that high school was going to be scary. Joining a small group when you've never been involved in a biblical community is similar to that first day of high school. This giant step in one's spiritual life is both exciting and scary.

Joining a core team after serving the group as a new member is akin to becoming a sophomore. You know how the high school works and while you're younger than some, you feel like a part of a family.

Leading out to spearhead group initiatives correlates to being a junior. You're not in charge, but you are making things happen and it feels good. Leading a core team to form a new group is akin to being a senior. With lots of team spirit, you are the starter on the football team or the lead presenter for the debate team.

Launching core-team-led small groups

If you believe the core team approach is what your small group ministry needs to succeed, the ministry itself must prove it's the right thing to do as you make changes in your routines and training to accommodate core teams.

Experiment with one group

By now you know how important it is to prototype anything new to sort out the obvious problems and ensure it takes hold in a healthy, organic way. Find one smaller group—eight members or less—led by a type B personality and members who have potential for success. Ask the leader if he or she would be willing to develop a team to lead instead of asking for volunteers. If the leader shows interest, invite him to read this chapter and talk with you about his ideas for forming a core team. The reason I recommend a smaller small group is for the sake of inclusion. A group of six or seven individuals will make a great core team and everyone can participate.

If I were you, I would join this group as a core team member. If others look to you to run the core team meetings or make all the recommendations because you're a pastor, tell them you have no idea what you're doing and should be considered the opposite of an expert or an authority figure. Take part in serving as any core team member would do, but don't share opinions and offer ideas during meetings when you could ask the group questions and support their solutions and plans.

My experience of being a core team member was illuminating. I clearly saw the kind of relational support the coach and pastor over my group required for success. Participation crystallized what our core teams needed when they were gathered for encouragement and training. I also enjoyed the extra time with my fellow group members and we bonded in a special way. Much like being on a team or a military unit, there's something powerful about joining forces with others to make things happen that no individual could achieve with volunteers.

Employ the first core team members

After a few months of core team leadership, invite the whole team to visit a leader's meeting to help you determine what should be changed to better support them. Meet with the core team promptly after the leader's meeting and ask them to comment on the content with questions such as: If all of our small groups were led by core teams, what changes would you make to our leader's meetings? What kind of initial training and ongoing support do core teams need from the church?

As they share, take copious notes. Follow up with anyone who throws a curve ball, sharing something you don't fully understand. What you are hearing is pure gold if you use the information to develop a support system for core teams.

Expand core-team-based groups

When the experimental group's core team has been successful, invite the leader to share his experiences with selected group leaders who are ripe for change. If the new group leaders show interest, work with them to form core teams and create working objectives for their meetings. The idea is to transition slowly so you can develop an adequate support system for core teams and their leaders.

The goal at this stage of transition must not be to shift all of your small groups to a core team approach. Focus on helping three or four of your groups grow through a core team approach and multiply. Then the balance of the groups will see the new approach is designed for growth and expansion and not just member involvement and reducing leader burnout.

Mobilizing every small group member for ministry

In a healthy small group, everyone involved should work toward success and help determine the direction of their group. Even with a fantastic leader, a group cannot grow and expand without the full participation of the members. By creating a core team that prays hard and makes plans to incorporate every member of the group, every member has the opportunity to be a minister with a ministry.

The core team-based approach also moves potential leaders through their training by living out the values of a group leader before they lead. Each core team meeting moves the participants from cognitive to psychomotor activity. As they find value and success in what they've executed, ownership increases and they're operating out of the affective domain. Best of all, every bit of this has occurred before they've been approached to lead a group!

As I watch new groups form at my church, the formal classroom training is not as important as the relationship between future leaders, their coach, and the small group pastor. We still offer the cognitive information through a training class, but our future leaders are learning so much about leadership from core team participation that it's not as important as it used to be. Visiting core teams and befriending the team member who is working hard produces leaders naturally.

American small group members do not envision themselves as future leaders compared to Christians in other countries. We have not set the bar too high for leadership, but too low for membership. Being a part of a biblical community requires active participation. Don't think that people don't want it. Everyone wants to be a part of the solution and on the winning team if given the opportunity. If your church doesn't have enough leaders for new groups, you're going about ministry the wrong way. Mobilize every member for ministry and develop leaders through team participation, not a training class. ◆

In the mid-1990s, I spoke to a woman named Daphne Kirk during a lunch break at a conference in England. While in line to receive our plate lunch, this total stranger turned to me and asked, "Why haven't you published anything on the role of children in group life?"

Flippantly, I replied, "Because you haven't written it yet!"

Little did I know I was speaking to a woman who had years of childhood development under her belt as an educator. If I were to seek out an author to write about how to empower children in small group ministry, she would have been my first choice. Without another word, we parted company and I forgot all about our verbal exchange.

Two years later, I received a package containing children's discipleship resources, guides for intergenerational groups, and a book introducing intergenerational small groups from a large publisher in England. To make a long story short, Daphne left the conference and started writing. An acquisitions editor for one of the U.K.'s largest Christian publishers heard about her work and published everything she submitted.

When it comes to writing about children in ministry and inter-generational small groups, I can't do the topic justice. I asked Daphne to share her heart concerning the biblical mandate for intergenerational groups and tips for integrating them into small group meetings, and she agreed. What you will read in this chapter is what she supplied, followed by my personal journey into intergenerational small group life.

CHAPTER SIX

The naked truth about intergenerational small groups: children are your most powerful small group members

by Daphne Kirk

As an increasing number of American churches express kingdom life through small groups, the place of children and families in the vision must be addressed. If small groups have biblical foundations, then the place of families and children can surely be found theologically. Biblically, only two mandates are given for raising the next generation: one generation is responsible for the next (Psalm 145:4); and parents are responsible for their children (Deuteronomy 29:29). These two simple commands would therefore imply that all of us are to be involved in raising the emerging generation.

Biblical examples of this can be found in Exodus 18 when Moses ordered the people of Israel according to the commands given by God to Jethro. In this passage, we see the child surrounded by family and the family by the community (tribe).

Acts 2:42-47 shows that when small groups met in homes with joyful celebration, children and families were caught up in the life of the body of believers, even if they fell asleep (Acts 20:9).

Children and families were involved in Jesus' life and ministry. There is no record of him setting the children on one side or ordering one of the disciples to run a nursery.

Throughout Scripture, words such as people, church, the whole community, everyone, and tribe are inclusive of every generation. Yet today the church interprets these terms to mean "adults." This digression from accurate biblical interpretation has resulted in drastic implications for centuries in the body of Christ, resulting in a church that operates in a similar way to a departmental peer-oriented education system. Peer learning is great for cognitive knowledge, but not for the development of the whole person. The question to ponder is: "Are you looking for small groups with big people, small groups with small people, or small groups with people?" To return to biblical truth, small groups must surely be for people of all ages.

> See, I will send you the prophet Elijah before that great and dreadful day of the Lord comes. He will turn the hearts of the fathers to their children, and the hearts of the children to their fathers; or else I will come and strike the land with a curse.   (Malachi 4:5, 6)

Today there is a cry for restoration of fathers (both natural and spiritual). Today God is pouring out his Spirit to turn a generation of fathers to a generation of children, and individual fathers to their children. The world in which this generation lives provides a serious wake-up call to every believer and every small group to prepare them "for such a time as this." One generation is responsible for the next.

We often pray for "his kingdom to come and his will to be done on earth as it is in heaven." Heaven is inclusive—every tribe and tongue—every generation all living and reigning, serving and worshipping together. May his kingdom come and his will be done on earth as it is in heaven in our small groups as well.

What do intergenerational small groups look like?

Where community is established by people who are committed to love God, love each other, and love the lost, members of different generations—including the single, elderly, children, families, parents, and grandparents—share life in communities that can be termed "intergenerational." We were created to live in an intergenerational environment, called family or community. Small groups should be a reflection of this and embrace that same culture.

Implications for families

The church preaches and teaches about godly families, worshipping, praying, and spending time in the Word together. Yet the message they give by their actions is that this is not possible. So few opportunities exist in the body of Christ where families can relationally experience kingdom community together! Generations meet together in joyful celebration to relationally celebrate events like birthdays, Thanksgiving, and Christmas, but also live together on a day-to-day basis and see this as normal. Why can't the church see this and provide it?

Throughout Scripture the generations (including families) gathered together (Exodus 18:6; 2 Chronicles 20:13; Nehemiah 12:43; Psalm 148:11-13; Matthew 19:13-15; Mark 10:15; Acts 2:42 -47) so children could learn in the lifestyle model of Deuteronomy 6:4-9:

> Hear, O Israel: The Lord our God, the Lord is one. Love the Lord your God with all your heart and with all your soul and with all your strength. These commandments that I give you today are to be upon your hearts. Impress them on your

children. Talk about them when you sit at home and when you walk along the road, and when you lie down and when you get up. Tie them as symbols on your hands and bind them on your foreheads. Write them on the doorframes of your houses and on your gates.

Each child is a unique and profoundly precious individual in the eyes of God. That individuality must be recognized within a community where they are known as individuals and where learning through generational modeling can take place. Holistic discipleship is best experienced in family or an intergenerational environment.

In Chapter 4, Randall eluded to an old African proverb: "It takes a village to raise a child." Let me use the proverb in a different way: where are the "villages" or the communities to raise the children of our nation who were "born for such a time as this?"

A vision for including the children

I was driving through our city this summer and saw children with teenagers, children and their parents, teenagers and adults in twos and threes, walking the streets. They were prayer walking together and delivering the "Jesus video" to homes as a part of a city wide initiative. I was moved as I realized that together they were taking the kingdom of God to people who desperately needed it.

I have heard children give powerful words to adults who have so desperately longed to hear the voice of God in situations. For example, some pastors were discouraged as they sought to develop small groups in the church. A child of about seven years went to them and said, "I think Jesus wants to say to you, 'Don't give up, even though people think you are silly . . . keep going.'" The pastor's wife cried because the message deeply touched her heart and soul. If children are empowered to minister to adults as well as other children, they will rise to the occasion.

Can we afford to miss the Word of God given so simply through children?
A small group was meeting and one member was absent with a migraine headache. The group's leader asked a child to pray for her. The child prayed, "Dear Lord Jesus, please make her better. Take away the pain and don't let her die. Amen." The adults laughed and spent some time reassuring the child that she would not die.

The next day, the leader called to see how the woman was feeling and spoke to her husband. "Haven't you heard? She has meningitis. But thank God, she did not die from it." A child does not dwell on logic but moves spontaneously by passing the logic of man to respond to the heart of God.

Can we afford to lose that role model from our lives?
In a restricted access nation, a small group of Christians gathered in a home, knowing the danger it posed for the homeowner and members. The police arrived, spat on a Bible and demanded each person deny Jesus or be shot in the head. A child stood up and wiped the Bible with her dress, saying, "Jesus, I am wiping the shame off your Word."

With that, she was killed.

Can we afford to remove a generation of children who will stand for Jesus even to martyrdom?
In many nations, children and young people are paying the price, standing for the sake of the gospel, speaking out, prepared to be

counted. They are praying where they are told they can't pray and speaking of Jesus where they are told to be silent. We cannot afford to underestimate or sideline their potential. If they can lay down their lives for the gospel of Christ, surely we can lay down our preconceived ideas and welcome them into our small groups!

The sound of thunder echoes over cities and nations as this generation revolts against the kingdom of darkness, releasing a victory shout of an emerging army. This is the generation of our children and young people. If we don't wake up to the challenge, if we put them out of our communities, if we don't realize their potential and embrace them, we will hand them over to others who will disciple them according to the world's values—through the media, music, education systems, advertising, and peer pressure.

1 Corinthians 12 unfolded

The youth cannot say to the elderly, "I have no need of you." The adults cannot say to the children, "I don't need you." The generation that seems to be the weakest is indispensable and the generation that we think is less honorable we treat with special honor. There should be no division in the body. Each generation should have equal concern for the other generations. If one generation suffers, every generation suffers with it. If one generation is honored, every generation rejoices with it. Now you are the body of Christ and each generation is a part of it. What God has joined together let no man separate!

What to do about it

How can we move into intergenerational small groups where every generation—including the children—is welcomed? For a deeper look, I recommend reading two books I've written previously on this topic entitled *Heirs Together* and *Reconnecting the Generations*. To whet your appetite, here are a few pointers, drawn from each book:

- Small groups are a biblical community, not just a meeting. Community is not neat and tidy, but relational and interactive.
- Invite your small groups to research and study biblical foundations that underpin intergenerational community (some of which have been outlined in this chapter).
- Prototype your first "intergenerational" small group with people who are enthusiastic and committed to the vision. Ideally, these people should be a mixture of singles, couples, and families. This group will serve as a model for others.

The following can be done within a small group or within your children's ministry to increase participation for members of all ages.

Always start newly formed groups with a Kid's Slot

A "Kid's Slot" is when the children go into a different room after the group has welcomed each other and enjoyed a time of worship. The children continue with the same theme as the adults, but in a separate room. On a rotating basis, group members can facilitate this time. In this way, children build relationships with all small group members, with each other, and with their heavenly Father; and they are empowered to reach their friends for Christ!

Use tested intergenerational small group materials

Until you know what you're doing, refrain from using your own material. Out of simple ignorance, many churches create material for the kid's slot or an intergenerational small group gathering that is too childish or too academic. Either will be inappropriate for both children and adults. When all ages are challenged and fruit is seen in every age group, then you will know that you have "pitched it" right. (The TOUCH web site has a number of excellent resources for intergenerational groups.)

Implement an intergenerational small group agreement and keep it operational

From the start, it is vital that the children and adults maintain ownership of what they have set out to be and do as a spiritual family. This agreement will touch on issues such as respecting the host home, responding to other members, discipline, and anything else where people might have differing standards and boundaries. Children should be encouraged to discuss these independently of the adults. Then the whole group should gather to compare ideas and reach an agreement. This agreement should be reviewed every two months during group meetings. By doing this, many unnecessary conflicts will be avoided.

Give children ownership of the group by asking their opinions and advice

By giving them an appropriate level of responsibility, the adults show faith for the children to move in the gifts of the Spirit and minister to other age groups. Everyone will benefit!

"As with adults"

Although children have special needs, the following principle makes it possible for anyone to facilitate an intergenerational small group. In any situation where someone is unsure what to do in relationship to a child, ask, "What would I do if an adult was in this situation?"

If a child is sick, visit him or her (as with adults); if a child does not want to go to the meeting, spend time talking with him to find out what the problem is (as with adults); if a child does not participate, break into pairs or triads so he or she can be drawn out (as with adults); and create an expectation that the children will be active participators of the small group (as with adults). In other words, disciple them, equip them, and empower them to reach the lost just as you would do with grown-ups.

The secret to moving a small group with childcare to an intergenerational small group is to treat the children the same as adults. By communicating with them between meetings to asking them to participate in ministry time, you will activate them early in life and everyone will reap the rewards.

Randall's take on intergenerational group life

As a coach, I love to visit my small groups. It's always a delight to drop in and participate. On one memorable occasion, I sat next to a nine-year-old boy in an intergenerational group. After sharing our answers to an icebreaker question and a time of kid-friendly worship, the children were released for their kid's slot (a special time for the ten-and-under crowd). During this time, the youngest children discussed what they were learning about God and prayed for each other while the tweens, teens, and adults spent time applying a Bible passage and ministering to one another.

The boy didn't budge, even though other children his age were bolting out of the room at the speed of lightning. When I asked him if he was going to stay in the meeting with us, he whispered, "God told me I'm supposed to pray for the old people tonight."

This little boy was a new Christian. In fact, his entire family had come to Christ just a month earlier and we were meeting in their home. Shortly after their conversion experience, the group's leader told the family members that they had the Holy Spirit within and to expect the Spirit to speak to them and direct them. Evidently this kid took that information very seriously. He had his game face on and wasn't about to leave the room, even when his friend urged him to go.

After everyone else received ministry, I shared with the group that I was exhausted from six weeks of coughing. The members, along with the boy, gathered around me to pray for healing. The first adult prayed, "Lord, if it is in your will that our brother be healed, let the medicine he's taken take effect." A woman prayed a rather standard prayer for healing she'd probably prayed a bunch of times, which sounded very human and not even heartfelt. Then the boy placed his hand on my chest and said, "Jesus, you died for this man and I know you didn't do that so he could be sick. Please heal him right now."

Holy heaven came over me when he said the word now. I felt God's power in such capacity that I choked back tears without success. The tightness in my chest was gone, and I took a deep breath. After I exhaled, the little boy said, "Mister, didja just get healed? I think you did!"

The room erupted in laughter. Then someone said, "I think we just had church!" and we laughed more. And on that miraculous note, the leader closed the meeting.

With my coach's hat on, I took the opportunity to ask the members to "unpack" what just happened so it could be repeated in the future. One adult said, "We've never really thought about asking our younger children to participate because we were sure they'd be bored." Another said, "I'd love to see my kids be in with us the whole meeting, but I was afraid they'd be disruptive and bother the other adults." Yet another parent said, "I'm on the other side of this. I don't feel comfortable sharing deep things with my children in the room … and others share things from time to time that are not appropriate for tender young ears."

Should kids be in?

Daphne and I have discussed this very issue at length. In a few small-group-based churches, we've both found that children are in the small group meetings the entire time and participate along with the adults. The parents treat the children as they would an adult member and invite them to share, pray for others, and receive ministry as well. The adults refrain from talking about sensitive particulars of a situation or confessed sin that would be inappropriate, but don't hold back otherwise. When Mom and Dad have been arguing all week, it's shared with the group so everyone—adults and children alike—can pray over them and break the strife. Their reasoning is that their children are smart enough to know that Mom and Dad are at war, even if the arguments have been made at low tones behind a bedroom door. Why cover it up? Discussing the need for help and receiving ministry shows the children that Mom and Dad care enough about their marriage to get help from their spiritual family.

When the children see their parents share transparently and those same children pray over their parents with other adults, something important has just been modeled. The children have just learned, "When I grow up and get married, I'm going to talk about my problems and get prayer instead of bottling it up as if it never happened."

Children do not see their parents share transparently and participate in the healing process when they are in Sunday school or kid's church. If they don't experience it in small group life, where will it happen? If it's happening at home, why is it not happening in their small group as well?

The Kid's Slot

As Daphne mentioned earlier, in many churches the small groups incorporate a Kid's Slot time after worship. This can be a great bonding time for adults and children in the group, but two or more adults will miss part of the meeting to make this work. (I recommend at least two adults to reduce the possibility of a child being mistreated in some way.)

Personally, I enjoy working with the children, but Etna and I don't have children so it's a big adventure for us. Some parents would rather not be a part of a small group if they have to take a turn working with the kids. The paradigm shift parents must make for intergenerational small group life is vastly different from the programmatic small groups found in churches today. The small group is not a spiritual "date night" for parents. A biblical community includes people of all ages, and all the participants have a full-sized Holy Spirit within them, regardless of height or age. Parents who refuse to work with the kids every six or eight weeks have yet to discover the power of ministering to the youngest members of the group and the benefits associated with it.

Children are the church of today

I do not believe that children are the church of tomorrow. If we do not include children in our biblical communities when they are very young, they will fall away from God and become a part of the world. Millions of twenty-somethings who grew up in age-segregated church programs have abandoned their faith. As adults, they never darken the door of a church. The segregated Christian education they received in the program-driven church did not make them the church of tomorrow.

The parents of these children were faithful to bring them to church every Sunday, where they participated in Sunday school or children's church. As they moved through puberty, the children joined the youth group and went on mission trips. The parents did everything the program-driven church told them to do and the children responded with full participation while living at home. Then they went off to college or into the workplace and forgot everything they were taught in the church's classrooms. The church focused on the cognitive domain and the head knowledge didn't make a dent in their worldly value system.

It would be easy to blame the degraded culture in which we live. No church program can compete with what children see on television, listen to on their iPods, read in text messages, are exposed to at school, or learn on the streets of their city or suburban neighborhoods. That's why introducing young children to the indwelling Christ and the activity of the Holy Spirit in an intergenerational environment is vital to their spiritual survival as they mature into adulthood.

In intergenerational small groups, I see the power of God moving through children in a way they rarely experience outside their own homes or in church buildings. When children are shown how to minister to adults (and other children) in the context of a biblical community, they are transformed into the church of *today*. Being a part of the church of today changes everything.

When a child discovers the power of the Christ within before he or she enters adolescence, teenage pregnancy and drug use are not a concern. The teen raised in an intergenerational small group has his or her sights set on ministry and fully serving the Lord, not the world.

The unadulterated truth about involving kids in meetings

Of all the challenges shared in this book, transitioning adult-only small groups to intergenerational biblical communities tops them all. In fact, it's as difficult to do as all the other things *combined*. Oddly enough, the challenge is not integrating the children, but reorienting the adults. The kids learn to minister to others and participate in group meetings and group life in just a few weeks. They're always up for something new. When they pray for someone—sensing the power of God surging through them for the first time like an adolescent or adult and receiving an encouraging word or seeing someone healed before their eyes—their lives become ministry-focused.

Introducing intergenerational small groups is an uphill battle with the parents. Most possess low expectations for child involvement beyond good behavior, which translates as remaining quiet and not being disruptive. Parents reel with fear when challenged to share deeply around their children, especially if they don't do it at home.

If you can successfully show the parents that raising their children "in a manner according to the Lord" includes showing them how to confess sin, receive ministry, love others unconditionally, suspend judgment, and serve selflessly in biblical community, you're on your way.

Keep the cart behind the horse

If you know intergenerational small groups are the future for your small group ministry, don't teach on the role of children and challenge parents to involve their kids. They're probably not ready for it unless you have a church dominated by home schooling families. Allow this to happen naturally or suggest it at the proper time.

Begin by asking group leaders (or core teams) to pray for the children of the group by name and relate to them directly outside of meetings. (Whenever I lead a small group, I call the children in the group to see how they're doing, pray with them individually, and ask them to pray for me in a specific area.) When the children respond and have that spark of interest in ministry (versus playtime) it's time to move to the next level: ministering to others alongside an adult. If someone in the group needs ministry, take a child from the group along.

By investing time with the children individually and involving them in ministry, they'll be ready to participate alongside adults in the small group meeting. This is where many churches fail. They do not show the children just how powerfully God can use them to minister to adults outside of meetings before they ask them to participate inside meetings. The meeting is the cart. Ministry to other children and adults outside of formal meetings is the horse that pulls the cart. If you keep this in mind, success will be yours.

At the appropriate time, ask the children if they would like to participate in ministry time with the adults. If they show interest, turn to the parents and ask them if they would be open to an intergenerational small group experiment. (I love the word *experiment*. It doesn't make the request sound as if it is a permanent change. If the experiment is successful, the group will determine how many future meetings should be intergenerational.)

By establishing a relationship outside of meetings and watching children in ministry blossom, the parents will be more open to including the children during meetings.

We must not lose another generation

The way Daphne and I see it, if a church values biblical community, it must value children enough to involve them in ways they've never experienced in traditional church life. We hope you feel the same way. If we don't show our children how to minister to others and be ministered to in our small groups, we will lose yet another generation. We must stop treating our children like the church of tomorrow by segregating them to teach them Bible stories and Christian values with a cognitive learning model. To release them to be the church of today, we must involve the youngest members of the church in every aspect of biblical community to activate a passion for ministry and co-labor with adults. If not, we will certainly lose our children and adults who have grown up void of fellowship with Christ or other believers. ◆

One day children were brought to Jesus in the hope that he would lay hands on them and pray over them. The disciples shooed them off. But Jesus intervened: "Let the children alone, don't prevent them from coming to me. God's kingdom is made up of people like these.

(Matthew 19:13-15, *The Message*)

CHAPTER SEVEN

The naked truth about small group-driven churches: guiding principles that produce healthy small groups

While I consult with pastors of struggling churches each day, I also relate to a number of church leaders who don't need the assistance of my ministry. The small groups in their churches are missional, producing conversion growth, discipling through mentoring, and the members are anxious to lead a group. They are my encouragement and give me great hope for the American holistic small group movement.

With my analytical hat placed firmly on my balding head, I've discovered these pastors and church bodies they serve are guided by a set of common ministry principles. While these principles are not extraordinary, the paradigm for ministry they provide when interwoven has everything to do with success for small-group-driven churches. As you read the last pages of this book, let each one sink down deep inside you to see what you can apply to bring organic growth into your small groups.

The leaders are motivated by their theology, not sociology

Last year I read a handful of new books that reveal a counterproductive motivation for small group ministry. One pastor wrote that adding fellowship groups is the primary way he's helped his church become "sticky." Evidently, small group involvement at his church reduces church shopping. Another pastor explained in great detail how to round up volunteer leaders, give them a crash course in leadership, advertise groups through the services, then move the entire congregation from the pews to living rooms. These pastors view small groups as an innovative way to give a typical consumer family that little something extra they want from church affiliation: actual relationships.

While small groups provide a depth of relational connection that the large congregational gatherings cannot provide, this is a lousy reason to launch groups. Filling a sociological hole in one's cathedral model with off-campus groups only creates a high maintenance program. Although the members of these groups are encouraged to reach up, reach in, and reach out, they know that showing up to meetings is all that is required to satisfy their basic relational needs. In reality, this kind of small group program has no missional thrust and therefore will never grow on its own.

Contrast this consumer-collecting view with the pastor who leads an interconnected network of organically growing holistic small groups. He has adopted a model of church that fully embraces the mandate for the priesthood of all believers.[1] In his mind, if you're not a member of a group, you are not a member of his church. After all, this is where ministry and mission are found. Faithful congregational attendance and tithing doth not a member make! His sermons are not designed to draw a crowd of individuals who have never met the people sitting nearby. Each week, he provides instruction and encouragement for what the small group members need for a deeper and more expansive ministry and welcomes the visitors brought by the small group members. If anything, congregational gatherings are viewed as supportive of the small groups, celebrating what the groups are achieving in a larger venue.

One such pastor is Lee Brockington, lead pastor of a growing small group-driven church in Katy, Texas called Life Church. If you were to visit with him, you would hear him unabashedly state, "We're raising up an army here, not an audience." Each year, his church cancels weekend services for one Sunday to reinforce that the church is genuinely rooted in small groups. On that weekend, if you don't visit a group, you haven't been to the lifeblood of Life Church. Like so many other successful small-group-driven church pastors, Lee values the congregational services for what they do for the groups. His church has harnessed the power of the large gathering to unify and magnify the ongoing ministry and mission in the small groups.

When you launch and expand your small group ministry because you know you'll never achieve your church's mission any other way, you're on the right track. Don't add groups to what you're currently doing because folks aren't connecting on a personal level. Discard the "come and see" model for the "send them out" model of holistic small groups. The members will develop a far deeper and transformational relational connection that grows and expands on its own with far less frustration.

The harvest is earned through relationships

The second principle found in these successful churches is their source of numeric growth. While some folks do come into these churches through the congregational gathering and are then enfolded into groups, the leadership does not view this as the primary point of entry. The pastors know that if the small group members are using friendship evangelism to love people into the kingdom of God and if these people are joining small groups, their churches will be a mile wide *and* a mile deep. So these pastors purposely keep the congregational services as a celebration of transformed lives through small group involvement and outreach.

When these churches offer a large harvest event such as a Christian concert, tickets are distributed through the small groups and the group members are encouraged to buy extra tickets for friends. The stimulus is not to draw a crowd of unchurched strangers, but to provide the small group members with a big event they could not provide on their own.

By refusing to mass-market a consumer-friendly model to the households around the church's property, these churches did not grow rapidly after they were planted and transfer growth remains minimal. (If numbers are important to you, you should know that eight of the ten largest churches in the world are small-group-driven. If you look at attendance charts for the first five or ten years, they had healthy growth of ten to twenty percent, followed by exponential growth as the members of the groups fully embraced the church's mission and ran hard with it.)

In small-group-driven churches, everyone who joins a group is a part of a team who sets goals for reaching friends for Christ. Within a few years, the conversion growth swells and the new believers don't fall away. They were reborn into a spiritual family who cares for them and they are compelled to participate in servanthood and become fully devoted followers of Christ.

When your small groups produce conversion growth through relational evangelism, you will discover a completely different kind of church emerge from within. The key to success is to be patient. Producing healthy groups takes time.

Every member is developed to mentor, not just be a minister

The third principle redefines the word *minister*. I come from a long line of preachers. Five generations of men in my lineage were ordained and pastored local churches. In my grandfather's era, *minister* meant a vocational preacher. In my father's era, *minister* meant every believer found in a church's congregation—even if they didn't provide ministry to anyone. (It was just a biblical truth that sounded great to shout from the pulpit.)

For the churches that have successfully embraced small group life as their missional thrust, *minister* translates into "one who mentors others." Ministers are people who are actually doing something to advance the kingdom of God and have spiritually mature offspring to prove it. Discipling others is a normal part of group membership in these churches.

The rewards of mentoring

No one can guarantee that the person into whom you are pouring your life will grow and become a changed individual. Balanced mentoring also includes others from the small group who support the one-on-one activity and keep both the mentor and disciple from taking too much from the relationship.

Another benefit of mentoring is that it keeps the mentor sharp and on a pathway to maturity. Lifelong mentors do not see group leadership, the role of a coach, or even the role of a full-time small group pastor or church planter as a hill they cannot climb. It's just the next natural step to take in relational ministry. This is especially true when children are involved in small groups and learn to serve and minister to others while they're still young. By the time they are teenagers, they hunger to plant campus churches or go into missions.

221

By redefining "minister" to produce a culture of mentoring and discipleship in your small groups, you will see your small group members become the driving force behind spiritual health and leadership development.

The lead pastors no longer call the shots

One of my buddies is a pastor of a rapidly growing church of healthy groups. In total transparency he confided in me, stating, "My people have taken the vision God gave me and have run with it so hard and so far that I wonder why I am still in my position. At times I feel as if I am following the small groups as a consultant or troubleshooter. It's not easy to keep up when the small group members are actually the church and not just showing up for it on Sunday morning."

In the cathedral model, the senior pastor is viewed as "the boss" by the staff and congregation, even if he doesn't want to be the boss and does not control his church. The traditional paradigm of the role has been forced upon him. Unless the missional thrust and center for ministry is decentralized and found in the small groups, he will always be considered the taskmaster. In a small-group-driven church, the pastor may initially run with the baton, but he hands it off to many others who expand the race in length, width, and depth. This is the fourth principle and it's a big one for both the lead pastor and the people he encourages and supports.

If you think you have big plans for your church, employ your members to evangelize, disciple, and pastor others through small groups. Elevate basic biblical community (small groups) to a place of prominence while diminishing other areas to show them you are serious about the shift. Focus the groups on prayer and heeding God's call on their lives. Over time, your small group members will prove that the creativity of the body of Christ is far greater than the dreams of one man or woman in charge.

It's all about Christ in the midst

A recurring phrase in this book is "experiencing the presence, power, and purposes of Christ in the midst." It is the single greatest thing that separates a successful church of organically growing groups from a struggling church *with* groups. Or, as my earthly father states it in Christ's Basic Bodies,

> The future of Christ's body will only continue as a New Testament movement when the groups are the Body of Christ and function as a basic Christian movement. The basic implementing unit of this movement must be God-made, Christ-indwelled and Spirit-empowered groups. The important issue is Christ. Does Christ show up in these groups as He promised? Is Christ in the midst of each group in divine presence, resurrection power and eternal purpose?[2]

My greatest takeaway from Dad's book was that all small groups begin as man-made groups. Everyone shows up with a personal agenda—whether they realize it or not—that must be surrendered to God. When the members gather in Christ's name and have nothing else on the list of things to accomplish, the group is spiritually transformed the way a caterpillar becomes a butterfly. In a God-made group, edification, ministry, healing, outreach, and a desire to birth a new group are signs that the members have successfully made the metamorphosis.

This is not an easy concept to explain. You simply have to

experience it to fully understand it. Therefore, others in your small group ministry must experience it to catch it and give it away. When you hear regular reports of your small groups having Upper Room experiences with God when they meet, organic growth will follow.

These churches pray!

The last principle found in every healthy small-group-driven church I've encountered (foreign or domestic) is a passion for prayer. The small groups devote large blocks of time to pray when they gather, and the lead pastor has been known to lead the congregation to pray instead of delivering a sermon as the Spirit leads. Members arrive at the church's facilities early on weekends to pray through the sanctuary while others take shifts praying around the clock for the church, the community, and the nations. Without exception, every church that has a healthy small group ministry has a healthy prayer life.

My friend Jim taught me a profound truth about prayer: "If you pray a little, you get a little power. If you pray a little more, you get a little more power. If you pray a lot, you get a lot of God's power." What a concept!

For your small group ministry to flourish and become a powerful force for building the kingdom of God, the members must pray *more*. Whatever level of prayer they have achieved can and should be exceeded. Challenge your groups to pray for an hour and let God capture their hearts. Give them topics to pray over and ask them to share God's replies with you personally. Invite them to walk the streets of their neighborhoods and pray for opportunities to connect with the people in the houses. Ask your small groups to invent and submit new ways and places to pray.

In other words, do everything and anything in your power to get your small group members and congregation as a whole to pray more than they do today. No one has ever reached the end of his or her life and said, "I wish I had not wasted the days of my life with all that adoration, confession, and intercession with God."

Slow down, get off the autobahn, and turn around

It was a crisp, clear morning in Frankfurt, and the first day of rest after two weeks of training small group leaders and preaching. Because it was my first visit to Germany, I was enamored with the thought of being behind the wheel of "the ultimate driving machine" on the autobahn. After breakfast, Etna and I went down to the rental-car office and signed the papers for the BMW I rented for a day trip.

To my delight, pushing the sport sedan to 140 MPH was every bit as exhilarating as I imagined. As you can guess, Etna was not thrilled about the speed I maintained. In fact, I think I heard her mumble something about rededicating her life to Christ! Her interest for the day was not riding with a speed freak, but exploring a very old German town with her loving, attentive husband.

Less than an hour into the drive, my beautiful copilot gave me what she thought was fair warning concerning our autobahn exit, but I overshot it. I also missed the next exit. And I missed the exit after that as well. After Etna provided a Sunday school lesson about safety and the main reason for our trip, I pried my lead foot off the accelerator and coasted to a pitiful 80 miles per hour. I then made a safe egress and a very humbling U-turn. For the rest of the journey, I drove at a speed that permitted extended views of wildflowers and hillside dairy farms. In other words, it was *painfully* slow but the right thing to do.

When we arrived in Rothenberg, we followed signs to a parking area outside the town itself, which was puzzling to say the least. I expected to drive into the center of town as we had done in Frankfurt. Seeing no automobile entrances after a trip around the town two times, we parked the car and walked through a small breezeway. On the other side of the wall, we discovered a pedestrian village void of modern automobiles.

How ironic. I viewed the day as an excuse to go fast, but quickly discovered it was about walking slowly hand in hand with my bride. Looking back, we should have rented the economy model Fiat and headed to a shoe store.

Slow it down there, partner

A friendly officer from Galveston issued me a citation this morning. According to his radar-gun display, I was driving 15 MPH over the posted speed limit. To avoid an insurance hike, I will sit through a full day of driver's education. And you can rest assured that I will be driving cautiously in the future, adhering to the speed limits posted along the roads I travel. America is not the place to drive fast.

My hope is that the information in this book has served as your citation to slow down and consider why you are doing small groups. If you will give them the priority and support they deserve, your members will become kingdom activists and your groups will grow from within.

For some churches, consumer-filled small groups will not immediately respond to this radical shift. Reorienting the members of the groups with prayer and relational evangelism will take time and possibly the need to start over with new groups. I've discovered there's nothing wrong with starting over when you have finally discovered

God's destination. I was humbled in Germany when I missed my exits repeatedly, and humbled again today when the officer pulled me over. God often humbles us so we can resume the journey at a safe speed and reduce the wear and tear on the vehicle and the passengers.

Is it worth it?

I will not lie to you. Abandoning an attractional cathedral model for a relational way of being the church will be the hardest thing you've attempted in ministry. Until the members of your church see themselves as minister with a ministry and a team with whom to accomplish it, the road will be filled with obstacles and unseen potholes. But when your members finally figure it out, win a friend for Christ, and disciple that person in a small group family environment, your church will seemingly change overnight. The transition may take months or years, but there's nothing slow about the transformation when it finally comes. In fact, it might take you by surprise and scare you a little. I certainly hope it does!

Enjoy the days of slow progress. Soon enough, you'll be holding on for dear life, wondering what on earth your small groups are getting into and how you will support their outrageous plans to be the church, not go to it on Sunday.

And that's the naked truth about producing a healthy, organically growing church of small groups. Get busy. ◆

Etna, thank you for your consistent support and patience. I don't know what I'd do without you, my love.

David and Bill, you are the best accountability partners a guy could have. Thanks for the Tuesday morning productivity questions and not-so-gentle prodding.

Jo and Becky, thank you for showing an old dog a new way of leading small groups with core teams.

Fellow Lifegroup members, thank you for keeping me young.

Mary and Ron, thank you for allowing me to rant about the book's content over your amazing home-cooked meals. By the way, can we have wings and hot sauce next week if I promise to be quiet?

Karl and Kathy, your friendship and support is a wellspring of refreshment to Etna and me.

Mike, thank you for all your editorial support and gentle comments about the content and how to improve it.

Scott, thank you for all those long phone calls of encouragement.

And finally, I must offer my gratitude to my lifelong friend John. You encouraged me to write when we were in our teens. Thank you for being my cheerleader.

Prayer Group Sample Agenda

Use this guide to pray with others for an hour, investing ten minutes in each of the topics. Make copies for each person in the room. As the facilitator, you should read the topic and the explanation for that topic and begin praying aloud immediately so others will join you in concert prayer.

Praise and adoration to your Creator

Begin your hour of prayer by praising God for his holiness and purity, which he freely shares with you through the shed blood of Jesus Christ. Thank him for his goodness and desire to bless you. Praise him for his patience and loyalty, even when you don't deserve it. Give him honor for the gifts and talents you posses, and be specific! Thank him for protecting you in ways you know about and those you will not know of until you meet him in glory. Finally, thank him for the privilege of being his representative in this dark and hurting world.

Pray for our federal government and its officials

As you pray for the U.S. Congress, Federal Court Judges, the President, and his cabinet, and other government officials, ask God to pour out his Spirit on each person or position. Use this time to intercede on their behalf, asking God to protect them, their families, and their relationships. Refrain from complaining to God about their positions on specific issues or party affiliation.

Pray for our city and your neighborhood

Take a few minutes to thank the Lord for this town and the things you love about living here. Praise him for the opportunity to be a positive influence on the many who live around us. Then, ask for a fresh understanding of how you can make a difference with your time, energy, and talents to make the people of our town feel loved and appreciated. Use the balance of your time to cry out to God for the unchurched in our town, asking him to give you a great awareness of their needs so you can respond in love.

Pray for safety in the schools in your area and the children that are taught there each day. Ask the Lord to bring to mind the businesses in your area and ask him to prosper each one. Then, pray for your neighbors by name, asking God for open doors to deepen relationships with them and serve them.

Pray for our church, the staff members, and their families

Pray for protection for our church. We're working hard to reach people for Christ and Satan is never happy about that. Ask God to protect the members, family units, small groups, and leadership. Take your time and think through each family, group, and lay leader and lift them up by name. We also need pray for the missional direction of the church as it moves forward, increasing relationships with one another, the Lord, and unchurched families in our community. Pray for each staff member by name and ask God to give them encouragement and joy in their work, peace in their families and homes, and wisdom as they serve God and the congregation.

Pray for your family

Petition God to be the kind of husband, wife, son, daughter, mother, or father that he would want you to be: slow to anger, quick to praise, full of wisdom, and to become a person of greater patience and grace. Thank God for each person in your family by name, highlighting one or two ways you see God shining through them, including skills, abilities, and talents.

Pray for the lost

Pray for deeper connections with unchurched friends, relatives, co-workers, fellow students, or neighbors. Thank the Lord for each person by name, highlighting one thing you love about that person. Then ask God for boldness with those you just prayed for and a new or stronger desire to tell them how Christ is working in you. (If you don't have any unchurched people in your life, use this time to ask God to show you the people on the landscape who are desperately looking for a friend like yourself.)

Pastor's Relational Survey

This informal survey's questions are predominantly based on Jesus' values compared to the actual relationships you have formed with your leaders and God the Father, not the ideals you hold about relational ministry. There's usually a gap between what we *think* we do and what we *actually* do. Answer based on your actions and it will reflect a current relational snapshot.

I highly recommend that you move through the questions *three times* with a fresh, blank copy of the survey. The first time, take it alone. Then take it with your spouse. Finally, give a blank copy to your key staff members and invite them to fill it out on your behalf (as if they were you) and privately discuss their answers.

I know that some who take this survey will not enjoy it, and it might make some people downright angry! The questions are very challenging, and it will be easy to take offense because I left out something important that you think is paramount to understanding your situation in life and ministry. Please note that this survey was designed to ask a set of questions about how relational your ministry is today and give you information for areas to work on for the future of your ministry. There is no scoring or points, just an opportunity to be brutally honest with yourself and others and become more relational as a pastor.

Jesus had twelve disciples, three of whom were considered his "inner circle." He spent lots of time with them to form relationships. As their relationships developed, he showed them who he was and involved them in his ministry, finally giving it to them and challenging them with the Great Commission. Dwell on what you know about Jesus' intimate relationships with his disciples, and answer these first few questions:

1. How many key persons would you consider to be your disciples today as indicated by a significant time investment?
   ❐ More than 12
   ❐ 12 or less
   ❐ None, I'm just too busy to disciple any of my leaders right now

2. "I know the concerns, hurts, and dreams of my disciples." How accurate is this statement for you?

❐ I know each of them intimately

❐ I know a majority of them intimately (65% of the total number or better)

❐ I know about half of them intimately

❐ I know a few of them intimately

❐ Not applicable (I chose "None" to Question 1)

3. How well do your disciples know you? This question pertains to those disciples with whom you have shared deep personal concerns, hurts, and dreams.

❐ If asked, all would say they know me intimately and they'd be right

❐ A majority (65% or better) know me intimately

❐ Half of them know me intimately

❐ Just a few know me intimately

❐ Not applicable (I chose "None" to Question 1)

4. How true is this statement: "I have so much administrative and office work and sermon prep time that it keeps me from relating to my leaders to a point of true intimacy."

❐ Very True. My admin/office/sermon prep work is so great that it has eliminated any ability for me to develop relationships.

❐ Somewhat True. My admin/office work is a sizeable load, but I find time to spend with my leaders. It's still unbalanced though.

❐ Not True. I focus a majority of my time and energy on relationships.

5. As you consider your answer to the question above, what do you think is the root issue?

❐ I am an introvert and don't like being around people all the time

❐ I just have too much admin/office work to do any "real" relational-based ministry in my position

❐ I don't have too much admin/office work. I'm just a poor manager of my time. If I were to be more self-disciplined and strategic...

❐ My reason is different from what you've suggested and none of the choices come close to my situation

❐ I answered "Not True" to the statement in Question 4

6. When I sit down to plan my day or week, I write down or mentally consider the names of the people I need to invest in before I list the administrative things I must do.

❏ True ❏ False

7. I regularly spend time "doing nothing" or relaxing and having fun with:

❏ Most of my leaders once a month individually (65% or better)

❏ Half of my leaders once a month individually

❏ One or two of my leaders once a month

❏ I don't have the time (or make the time) to have friendships with my leaders

8. I spend the following amount of time in devotional prayer each day, on average:

❏ 15 minutes ❏ 30 minutes ❏ 45 minutes

❏ 1 hour ❏ 2+ hours ❏ I do not pray consistently every day

9. Is a daily time of prayer written into your job description?

❏ Yes ❏ No

10. Do you pray daily for your leaders with knowledge of their specific personal needs)?

❏ I pray daily as described with specifics

❏ As described, consistently 5-6 days a week

❏ As described, consistently 3-4 days a week

❏ As described, consistently 1-2 days a week

❏ I pray for the leaders I serve on occasion

❏ My prayer are surface level and sporadic

11. In the last 12 months, I have taken my staff and/or core lay leaders on a retreat.

❏ No

❏ Yes, as a reward (no teaching, just fun activities or relaxation)

❏ Yes, as a reward *and* to train them for ministry

❏ Yes, as a training time (not perceived by participants as a reward or primarily a "fun" time, but it was relaxing!)

12. "I hold my staff pastors accountable in the area of time investment with those they serve as their first job responsibility." How would your staff respond to this comment, made about you?
    ❐ My staff would say this is true for me. Each week I expect them to report on how they invested into the lives of others, not how many hours they were in the office.
    ❐ My staff would say I only hold them accountable for getting their administrative and Sunday-morning prep work done, so it would not be not true in their opinion.

13. "I have a godly balance between my family life and my ministry life." If married, how would your spouse respond to this statement?
    ❐ My spouse would say I spend quality balanced time with the family
    ❐ My spouse would say I don't spend enough time with the family

14. "I have a godly balance between my family life and my ministry life." If you have children, how would those who still live at home with you respond to this statement?
    ❐ My children would say I spend quality time with them regularly
    ❐ Most or all of my children would say I don't spend enough time with them, and the church seems to get most of my energy

15. If married, do you have a date night with your spouse?
    ❐ Weekly, and it's a huge priority
    ❐ Once or twice a month, and I don't let other things get in the way
    ❐ Date night? I'd love to, but I have no time for it now

16. Do you have a hobby or non-church-related activity that you enjoy with regularity?
    ❐ True. I enjoy this hobby or activity alone
    ❐ True. I enjoy this hobby or activity with at least one staff member, buddy, or family member as often as possible
    ❐ False. Ministry is just too encompassing to have a hobby or activity right now

17. Are you a vital part of a small group where you *actively* share, serve, minister to others, and receive ministry?
   ☐ True   ☐ False

18. Do you have an accountability partner with whom you meet regularly and are totally honest with him about your struggles, thought life, habits, and the state of your spiritual disciplines?
   ☐ True   ☐ False

20. Do you have friendships with lost or unchurched persons?
   ☐ I spend at least two hours a week or more with a lost person, just being a good friend
   ☐ I spend on average one hour a week with a lost person
   ☐ I spend a couple of hours a month with a lost person
   ☐ I do not have one unchurched person in my life who would call me his or her friend

What's Next?

If you haven't taken the survey with your spouse, print a blank copy and go through each question. You may be surprised how he or she responds. Then ask your key leaders or staff members to answer the questions that pertain to them and challenge them to be honest with you.

You'll most probably find areas that need work. Take time to visit with your family, staff, and leaders and involve them in the process of helping you discover ways to be more relational in ministry.

Sample Boot Camp Outline
(taken from Life Basic Training *by Ralph W. Neighbour, Jr.)*

Session 1: Are we significant?

Our real significance. Luke 10:38-42 is explored, challenging the person to identify with Mary or Martha and examine his or her sense of worth.

Session 2: Is what we do significant?

The father's single request: be his servant or administrator among men. 2 Peter 3:9; Matt. 28:18-20; Luke 4:18-19, 12:42; and Acts 3:1-8 are explored to help the person see how and why they are to serve God.

Session 3: Is what we do the result of who we are?

The story of the prodigal son is explored (Luke 15:11-32), giving the person a better perspective of God's desire to renew a relationship that is transforming. This sessions plants seeds for caring about those who do not yet have a relationship with God.

Session 4: Are sons also servants?

Servanthood is not an optional. Matt. 10; Isaiah 53:6; and Luke 9:1-9 are explored to find that God has given us his power and it must be used responsibly. The text goes on to explain God's power in us should bring peace to close friends, family members, coworkers, or fellow students.

Session 5: What makes serving so significant?

Friendship: The servant's reward. John 15:15-16, 26-27, 16:24; Col. 4:7-14; and Rom. 10:13-15 are used to show the person his friendship with God and other believers (biblical community) is special and powerful.

Session 6: Jesus speaks about servanthood

The value of Jesus. Matt. 9:36-38, 20:25-28; Mark14:3-7; John 11:25-26; and Phil. 2:3-8 expose Jesus' values: status, wealth, right to happiness, how he viewed his life, and how he viewed people in particular and mankind in general. This session also sets up the next one, inviting the person to write down twelve things they want to accomplish in life, keeping God's will in mind.

Session 7: The making of a servant: Moses, the "somebody"

Actualizing your dreams. Gen. 13:15-18, 15:1-6; Num. 13:31, 14:6-9; and John 9:4 guide the person to dream about accomplishing big things with God the way he used Moses.

Session 8: The making of a servant: Moses, the "nobody"

The call of Moses. Ex. 3:1-22, 4:1-9, 10-12; and Acts 7:22 shows the person that there is no excuse to avoid servanthood because one does not feel significant in the eyes of man.

Session 9: Moses' rejection of God's commission

Complete your committent. Luke 4:5-8, 8:15 and Phil. 1:6, 3:17, 4:11-13 move the person to remain faithful to servanthood when times get tough.

Session 10: Moses becomes the servant of God

Wired for power. Mark 9:17-24; Acts 3:1-11, 4:4; and Ex. 4:1-7 are studied to show God's power to heal the sick and the danger of unbelief.

Session 11: The "Segullah" people

Priestly living. Rom. 9:1-3, 10:1; Heb. 13:15-16, 1 Thes. 2:8; and Rev. 1:5-6, 5:9-10, 20:6 bring the person into an understanding that he or she is a "special treasure" (*segullah*) and a priest who represents men before God and make sacrifices to serve.

Small Group Leader's Self Assessment

The most exciting thing in life is to see people being changed, especially when you know you could never have changed those lives. Wow! We have a wonderful God. God changes people when they care for one another. Leading a group will prove to be one of your most rewarding experiences in ministry. To see God move through your group and your leadership will transform your life. In fact, as you lead others, you will discover that your life will be changed even more than those who follow you.

Leadership is a journey you will never complete because you can always improve in one or more areas. Moreover, the traits of effective leadership can be developed. Ninety percent of your leadership abilities are developed practices or habits. The remaining ten percent is comprised of personal leadership gifts. These gifts will only succeed if a person develops the other ninety percent. If you do not develop and practice the habits of effective leadership, your unique giftings will lie dormant. You can grow to be a good leader. The holy spirit is within you to help you. Your church has pledged to develop you. Your pastor and coach are committed to your success. The only things that others cannot give you are a desire to learn and persistence in growing. If you supply the desire and you choose not to give up, you will succeed.

While this self-assessment is designed to help you lead a small group of people into ministry and mission, the things that you will learn in it will help you be a better leader in all walks of life. You cannot avoid being a leader. Sooner or later, you will have to lead others—whether in your family, work, society, or church. The only question is what sort of leader you will be. This guide is only a tool to help you develop as a leader.

You need your coach. A coach helps you develop as a small group leader and mentors you as you learn the practices of an effective leader. This person might be your current small group leader, your pastor, or another leader in your church. As you enter into leadership, learn as much as you can from your coach. Don't be afraid to share openly with him or her and discuss what you are learning about yourself and others.

Are you ready? Here we go! Have fun while you grow!

Your relationship with God

1. Briefly describe how you initially came to know christ as lord and savior. How would you describe your relationship with God?
   ❒ Exciting — I have a close walk with God
   ❒ Rollercoaster — I feel close to him, but at times I feel he is far away
   ❒ Committed — I am mentally dedicated, but my heart wavers
   ❒ Faith-building — I know God loves me, but I don't always feel it
   ❒ Tough — I struggle in obeying God; I find it hard to obey at times
   ❒ Other: _____

2. Describe a recent experience with God that illustrates why you checked the box above:

3. How many days in the last week did you have a quality personal time with God? _____

4. Please share one significant experience you had in your personal time with God from the last week:

Your ministry involvement

5. What ministry training have you completed? (Check all that apply)
❐ A basic discipleship course ❐ A spiritual gifts course
❐ A worship-leading course ❐ A relational evangelism course
❐ A mentoring course ❐ Small group leader training
❐ Other:_____

6. In what area of small group ministry have you participated?
❐ Leading worship in small group
❐ Leading the icebreaker in your small group meeting
❐ Following-up with a new believer
❐ Caring for a small group member
❐ Leading the prayer time in the small group meeting
❐ Praying for someone during the small group meeting
❐ Organizing a small group activity
❐ Bringing new people to the small group
❐ other: _____

7. List the ministry activities in which you have been involved in the past.
(Check those in which you are currently committed):
❐ _____ ❐ _____
❐ _____ ❐ _____
❐ _____ ❐ _____
❐ _____ ❐ _____

8. List the names of 3-5 people you have had a significant influence upon for Christ:

9. Who was the last person you played a significant role in leading to Christ?

10. Briefly describe a time when God used you to minister to someone in great need:

11. Have you ever personally discipled another person who went on to effectively disciple other people?   ❒ Yes   ❒ No

12. Who? _____

13. Think of a time when you feel you were especially effective at encouraging another person. Briefly write about that experience:

14. In a time when you have found being a leader a great challenge, how did you handle it?

15. Who is the last person with whom you formed a close friendship?

16. Think of a time when you committed to a task and uncontrollable circumstances interfered with your ability to complete that task. What did you do?

17. How well do you know the people who live near your home?
    ❏ We are good friends and spend time together often
    ❏ We are not close friends, but I am actively developing a friendship
    ❏ I know their names, and we visit casually now and then
    ❏ We say "hi" when we see one another
    ❏ I do not know my neighbors and rarely see them
    ❏ Other _____

18. Describe a recent encounter with a neighbor that was significant:

19. Describe what happened the last time you entertained people in your home:

When no one is looking

20. Think of a recent time when you were transparent with others. Was it a positive or negative experience? What made it so?

21. In a recent experience of feeling lonely, how did you respond?

22. Briefly describe a situation where you used your financial resources to benefit someone else. How did you feel doing this?

23. Think of the last time you experienced spiritual failure (sin). How did you respond?

24. In a recent experience where you underwent strong temptation, how did you handle the situation?

25. Consider the last time you relocated to another city. What were your primary reasons for making the decision?

26. Think of a recent major decision. Describe what you did to arrive at the decision you made.

27. Think of a recent time when you did not get your way. How did you respond to the situation?

Your availability for ministry to others

28. Think of a time when you were asked to accept a responsibility you felt you did not have the time or energy to do. How did you respond?

29. Is small group leadership a responsibility that you think you have enough time and energy to do?   ❐ Yes   ❐ No

30. If married, is your spouse supportive of your involvement in small group ministry?   ❐ Yes   ❐ No

30. If you answered "no" to the last question and you feel God is calling you to lead a group, how will you adjust your life?

A process for refocusing your priorities

Step 1: Write down the various activities to which you have made
commitments (your job, children' s activities, hobbies, social
events, etc.)

❒ _____   ❒ _____

❒ _____   ❒ _____

❒ _____   ❒ _____

❒ _____   ❒ _____

Step 2: Check those activities that are God's priorities. If you don' t
know, ask the Lord to show you.

Step 3: Of the ministry activities checked on page 243, which of those
do you feel a specific call of God to do? (Again, ask the Lord to
show you.)

Step 4: With whom do you need to discuss the changes in priorities
you feel the Lord leading you to make (spouse, pastor, children,
boss)?

Step 5: Make a plan to change your priorities. (The following questions
will prove helpful to forming your plan of action.)

Your relationship with leadership

31. How do you regard the vision and strategy of your church? (Check all
    that apply.)
    ❒ I support the entire vision with my attendance and financial backing
    ❒ I believe in the vision but am not as involved as much as I would like
    ❒ I question the vision, but I participate in it anyway
    ❒ I question the vision, and I discuss my concerns with others
    ❒ I do not believe in the vision of the church
    ❒ I do not know the vision of my church
    ❒ Other: _____

32. Think of a time when you disagreed with the vision or strategy of a
    church you were involved in. How did you respond?

33. How do you respond to spiritual authority?
    ❒ Blind obedience. I obey without giving much thought to it
    ❒ Honestly. I contribute thoughts and follow my leaders completely
    ❒ Trustfully. I trust leadership even though I don't always understand
    ❒ Questioning. I often find myself harboring doubts and questions
      about spiritual leaders
    ❒ Reluctantly. I follow spiritual leaders, but I find it difficult to trust
    ❒ Independently. I prefer to work alone and be led by what I feel God
      is showing me
    ❒ Other: _____

34. Think of a time when you were in conflict with someone in spiritual
    authority over you. How did you respond?

A good leader is a good servant

Jesus taught us: *"you know that the rulers of the gentiles lord it over them, and their high officials exercise authority over them. Not so with you. Instead, whoever wants to become great among you must be your servant, and whoever wants to be first must be your slave — just as the son of man did not come to be served, but to serve, and to give his life as a ransom for many"* (Matthew 20:25-28).

As you move into group leadership, you will be one of those working the hardest and serving the most. For a Christian leader, servanthood is a big responsibility, but it is the greatest privilege. By becoming a servant, you are becoming more like our Lord, and he has pledged that he will serve those who serve others for his sake (Luke 12:37).

There are characteristics of a servant:
• A servant leads. The greatest servants are the greatest leaders. They model the life of christ for others and lead people into servanthood.
• A servant does menial tasks. A servant does not pick and choose what he will do. He does what needs to be done, even the most menial tasks.
• A servant is faithful. God looks for faithfulness in his servant. Faithful means *reliable*. You can count on the person to carry out the instructions given quickly and thoroughly.
• A servant sees the need. He does not need to be told. A good servant takes the initiative and does whatever has to be done.
• A servant is diligent. In all of Jesus' teachings and through his own example, he demands that a servant work hard. A good servant does more than he is asked.
• A servant is available. When the need arises, the servant is ready to serve. He is prepared to do service at all times.

35. Rate yourself on a scale of 1 to 10 (10 being the highest):

A servant leads	1	2	3	4	5	6	7	8	9	10
A servant does menial tasks	1	2	3	4	5	6	7	8	9	10
A servant is faithful	1	2	3	4	5	6	7	8	9	10
A servant sees the need	1	2	3	4	5	6	7	8	9	10
A servant is diligent	1	2	3	4	5	6	7	8	9	10
A servant is available	1	2	3	4	5	6	7	8	9	10

Be a proactive learner

"My son, if you accept my words and store up my commands within you, turning your ear to wisdom and applying your heart to understanding, and if you call out for insight and cry aloud for understanding, and if you look for it as for silver and search for it as for hidden treasure, then you will understand the fear of the Lord and find the knowledge of God" (Proverbs 2:1-5).

There are three types of learners:
• The unresponsive learner. This person is not open to learn. This person feels they know enough or everything there is to know.
• The passive learner. This person will learn if taught, but he or she is waiting for someone else to take the initiative.
• The proactive learner. This person seeks to learn new things and grow even if no one is teaching him or her. This person will find someone to teach him because he is hungry to learn and needs the help of another.

If you develop a proactive learning spirit, it will bless you for the rest of your life. The moment you stop learning, you will become a grumpy old person!

36. Proactive learners have certain qualities. Rate yourself on a scale of 1 to 10 (10 being the highest):

Spending time with God each day	1 2 3 4 5 6 7 8 9 10
Reading stimulating books	1 2 3 4 5 6 7 8 9 10
Seeking input from others	1 2 3 4 5 6 7 8 9 10
Asking questions	1 2 3 4 5 6 7 8 9 10
Learning new ways of doing things	1 2 3 4 5 6 7 8 9 10
Trusting the direction of my leaders	1 2 3 4 5 6 7 8 9 10

What's next?

With your coach, pastor, or small group leader, review your answers and record the areas of life and ministry that need attention to grow as a leader.

Chapter One

[1] A.W. Tozer, *The Counselor*, (Camp Hill, Christian Publications, 1992), 112, 113.

[2] Larry Stockstill, *The Cell Church* (Ventura, CA: Regal Books, 1998), 22.

[3] Stockstill, 18.

[4] Larry Stockstill served as a TOUCH Outreach Board Member for three years in the mid-1990s, making valuable contributions to my ministry's direction.

[5] William Hendriksen and Simon J. Kistemaker, *Vol. 5: New Testament Commentary: Exposition of Philippians* (Grand Rapids, MI: Baker Book House), 121.

[6] *Barna Update*, March 14, 2006.

[7] Neil Cole, *The Organic Church*, (San Francisco, CA: Jossey-Bass, 2005), 31, 32.

[8] "Kingdom Activist" is a term I coined to clarify what many would call a kingdom *seeker*. In the deceived mind of a consumer Christian, they truly believe they are seeking the kingdom of God when in fact, they only have ideals to support this belief. By definition, an *activist* is one who takes vigorous action to bring about social change. This is what Christ has called us to do. Not *think* about doing it, but *actually* doing it, even if we have no support or no idea what we're doing.

[9] Praying aloud and simultaneously is not a Pentecostal or charismatic practice. If you have never prayed in this way in a small group setting, I encourage you to experiment with it to discover a far more powerful time of corporate prayer.

Chapter Two

[1] Ralph W. Neighbour, Jr., *Where Do We Go From Here?* 1st Edition, (Houston, TX, TOUCH Publications, 1990), 431.

[2] This information and many other excellent data can be found in Dr. Egli's doctoral dissertation. Visit his ministry's web site for more information: http://www.smallgroupsbigimpact.com

[3] Cole, *Organic Church*, 95.

[4] The average pastor invests two days per work week developing his sermon.

[5] http://www.joelcomiskeygroup.com/articles/churchLeaders/CellDrivenChurch.htm.

[6] Volunteerism is helping a church do something for free or without expectation of being paid or repaid. This is vastly different from surrendering to God's call on one's life to become a minister and a home missionary, the two terms that best describe a healthy holistic small group member.

[7] After writing about the Mary and Martha group analogy I came across a similar reference in Bill Beckham's writings. However, he uses it in a different way as it pertains to cell groups. Check out *The Second Reformation* for more information.

[8] Before a person could proceed with this online survey, they were asked two qualifying questions. The first was to determine that they were the lead or senior pastor of their congregation. The second was to ask the pastor if he and his church were fully committed to transitioning away from programs to become a cell-group-based church (or what many call holistic small groups).

[9] D. Michael Henderson, *John Wesley's Class Meeting: A Model for Making Disciples* (Nappanee, IN: Evangel Publishing House), 138.

[10] M. Scott Boren, *The Relational Way*, (Houston, TX, TOUCH Publications, 2007), 42-43.

[11] M. Scott Boren, *How Do We Get There From Here?* (Houston, TX, TOUCH Publications, 2007), 169-170.

[12] If you have not read *Refrigerator Rights* by Dr. Will Miller, I highly recommend it. It remains one of the most life-changing books I have ever read, and reveals why American Christian are ineffective in relationships.

[13] Neighbour, p.61.

Chapter Three

[1] Rick Warren stated the following at both the 2007 and 2008 Saddleback Small Group Conferences in which I was an attendee: "We tell our people, if you know how to use a vacuum cleaner and a DVD player, you can lead a small group."

[2] The NCD Survey measures the health of a local church. Based on the research of the Institute for Natural Church Development in 40,000 churches, it helps a church identify areas of strength and weakness. On the basis of this, a growth plan is developed that leverages a church's strengths to shore up weak areas. Learn more about it from the organization's web site: http://www.ncd-international.org/public/profiles.html.

[3] Any staff member appointed to be the small group champion must be freed from his or her previous duties. Rewrite his job description and transfer responsibility for traditional church-program involvement to others.

[4] http://en.wikipedia.org/wiki/Fibonacci_number.

Chapter Four

[1] http://evotional.com/2008/06/random-firings-of-synapses.html.

[2] George Barna, *Growing True Disciples*, (Colorado Springs, CO: Waterbrook Press, 2001), 46, 47.

[3] Alpha is a facilities-based evangelism program designed in the U.K. and used all over the world to help unchurched people speak openly about their beliefs in a non-threatening environment after watching a video containing biblical truths about many basic issues. To learn more, visit http://www.alpha.org.

[4] Ephesians 4:14.

[5] Larry Kreider, *Authentic Spiritual Mentoring*, (Ventura, CA: Regal, 2008), 14.

[6] Ephesians 4:11, 12.

[7] Matthew 28:18-20.

[8] Ralph W. Neighbour, Jr., *The Arrival Kit* (Houston, TX: TOUCH Publications, 1993), 14.

[9] Dave Earley, *8 Habits of Effective Small Group Leaders* (Houston, TX: TOUCH Publications, 2001), 40.

[10] Barna, 47, 48.

[11] Dennis McCallum and Jessica Lowery, *Organic Disciplemaking* (Houston TX: TOUCH Publications, 2006), 39.

[12] Ibid, 61.

[13] If the person has not made a full or public commitment to Christ, the mentor is encouraged to listen as the person commits his or her life to Christ in prayer. Just before the event concludes, the disciple is presented to the group as a new believer and water baptism is scheduled.

[14] If you've never seen The Journey Guide for New Believers by Ralph Neighbour, you should review it to see if it will work for your discipleship process. It's a simple self-assessment tool that is inexpensive compared to other instruments, yet highly effective for starting tough conversations.

[15] I personally use a little book my dad wrote years ago called Beginning the Journey. It covers the basics, and by the time they're done with the five weeks of daily growth guides, my disciples are anxious to go on a freedom weekend to find freedom from strongholds.

[16] I have interviewed lead pastors from some of the most effective disciple-making small-group-based churches overseas and as well as churches in the United States. Without speaking to other pastors, each one concluded that every new believer needs "soul therapy" or deliverance as soon as possible after conversion. When I asked them if they could disciple people effectively without it, I was told that they added it to their pathway after they

discovered their mentors could not walk the disciples through a deliverance process consistently or quickly. Without a freedom encounter or deliverance retreat, they reported their mentor-driven discipleship process was not effective or reproducible.

[17] Neil Anderson's ministry, Freedom in Christ, as well as my own ministry, TOUCH Outreach, offer excellent resources. The major difference between the two as I see it is that Anderson's material is a truth encounter and TOUCH's resource is a truth and power encounter. Review both and decide which one works best for you. Then redesign whatever you choose to make it work more effectively for your disciples after repeated use.

[18] Philippians 2:12.

[19] *The Arrival Kit* by Ralph Neighbour, Jr. is a solid resource for this second part of the journey, but many others are also available from a variety of sources. What makes a discipleship resource transformational has far more to do with the disciple's willingness to change and the support of his or her mentor than the actual content of the resource (I find most cover the same topics). I look for resources that are designed to move the user to action through writing out their answers to questions and doing activities.

[20] Supplying each group with a *Blessing List* is a wonderful way to foster discussion and prayer at the event and in subsequent small group meetings. I'll discuss how to use the Blessing List later in this chapter.

[21] Paul R. Ford, *God is Powerful In You*, (Houston, TX: Cell Group Resources, 2008), 5.

[22] Do not rush ahead if you and at least two of your team members cannot reach someone for Christ with the principles of relational evangelism. Struggles and breakthroughs in the process of relating to unchurched and lost persons is the best foundational experience for mentoring that anyone can receive.

[23] The greatest person in any group and the one most admired is the one who serves (Luke 22:24-27). Potential mentors will view a young believer with a servant's heart as someone they could easily mentor.

[24] Without relational evangelism, I do not believe you will be able to successfully implement a discipleship pathway that takes root and becomes part of the DNA of your small group ministry.

[25] You can make your own with a roll of butcher paper or purchase pre-printed Blessing List posters from www.touchusa.org. I've found the preprinted posters are more frequently used than the homemade variety.

[26] Excerpt from an email dated August 18, 2008.

Chapter Five

[1] Email correspondence from April 10, 2009.

Chapter Six

[1] 1 Peter 2:9.

[2] Ralph W. Neighbour, Jr., *Christ's Basic Bodies* (Houston, TX: TOUCH Publications, 2009), 35.

Additional Resources by the Author

Community Life 101: Getting the most out of your small group experience

This pocket-sized book was written specifically for small group members who are new to a small group (or who are already in a group), yet have no experience to know how it differs from traditional programs like Sunday School or a Bible study. Written with numerous stories of true small group experience, this easy-to-read book has short chapters on the following topics: Spending time with God and other group members between meetings; Involving unchurched friends and family members in the activities and relationships of the group; Seeing yourself as a future group leader; How to be a powerful minister to others during meetings, and more.

A Pocket Guide to Coaching Small Groups:
Befriending leaders and helping groups produce fruit

Are your coaches busy people who don't have time to read? This book is small but will have a big impact on your coaches! Through stories and humor, the author shows coaches how to be a genuine friend of both the leaders of their groups and future leaders. Makes an excellent gift.

The Answer Book for Small Group Leaders

This pocket book contains hundreds of answers to frequently asked questions about small group life and leadership. Topics include: how to approach an over-talker; ministering to hurting persons by maintaining healthy boundaries; moving a group beyond the conflict stage; what to add when an unbeliever visits a meeting; and much more.

303 Icebreakers: hundreds of ways to break the ice in your group!

Questions range from light hearted to deeper questions about one's dreams and hopes in life. Questions are organized into the stages of a group's maturity for fast selection. Every small group leader should have a copy of this little book. Makes a great gift at Christmas time or when a new leader starts their group.

The Blessing List Prayer Poster (22 x 34 inches)

Help every small group in your church keep outreach a priority with this simple and inexpensive tool. Each member supplies two names for the list, which is posted by the host in the room where the group gathers. Contains instructions and the principles of relational evangelism shared in this book.

Each of these resources is available in quantity at a substantial discount off retail

Visit the publisher's web site to order these resources: www.touchusa.org
Or, call this toll free number: 800-735-5865